TILDA'S STUDIO

TILDA'S STUDIO

Tone Finnanger

Over 50 fresh projects for you,
your home and loved ones

David and Charles
www.rucraft.co.uk

Contents

A DAVID & CHARLES BOOK
© Cappelen Damm AS 2011
www.cappelendamm.no
Originally published in Norway as *Tildas Atelier*

First published in the UK and USA in 2011
by F&W Media International, LTD

David & Charles is an imprint of F&W Media
International, LTD
Brunel House, Forde Close, Newton Abbot,
TQ12 4PU, UK

F&W Media International, LTD is a subsidiary
of F+W Media Inc.
4700 East Galbraith Road, Cincinnati,
OH 45236, USA

A catalogue record for this book is available
from the British Library.

ISBN-13: 978-1-4463-0158-6 paperback
ISBN-10: 1-4463-0158-3 paperback

Printed in China by RR Donnelley
for F&W Media International, LTD
Brunel House, Forde Close, Newton Abbot,
TQ12 4PU, UK

10 9 8 7 6 5 4 3 2 1

F+W Media Inc. publishes high-quality books
on a wide range of subjects. For more great
book ideas visit: www.rucraft.co.uk

Welcome to Tilda's Studio

I have so much passion for my work (except for accounting and office work) that, in my house, work and personal life blends into each other. My job is to do what I love to do most in this world, and I have to remind myself every day how lucky I am.

When I am working in the studio, I make simple displays to get an idea of how projects will look when they are put together. I allow myself to be quite bold with these displays. This book is inspired by my workroom and each chapter is inspired by one of my displays. Maybe they will give you some new ideas?

I hope there is something for every taste in here.

A difficult year has passed. In March something happened that wasn't supposed to happen – my dear mother was taken away by a remorseless disease. She loved life and fought bravely to get more time. She has been my support and best friend through all these years with Tilda and life in general. She followed every detail with an interest only a mother can have. She was intelligent, well-informed, considerate and unceremonious, and I was extremely proud of her. It meant a lot to me to experience unconditional love from such a great person.

I can't write this preface without thanking her for everything I am. Without her believing in me I never would have dared to.

Many of you know how creativity can help lighten your mood. Tilda and this book have without a doubt helped me through a difficult time in my life. You have to fill those moments with what you like most and remember to enjoy life.

Tone Finnanger

Materials

Tilda materials and fabrics are mainly used for the projects in this book. The Tilda Face Painting set is used to make faces on all the figures. Tilda hair comes in four different colours; dark brown, red brown, blond and white. To make a fringe, there is an embroidery yarn to match the three first colours.

Plain-dyed fabrics are used for skin and wings. Dark skin-coloured fabric is used for the angels, light skin-coloured fabric for the giraffes, sand colour for the elephants and white for the cockatoos. Light pink fabric is used for the angel wings.

Patterned fabrics and ribbons are from the Tilda collecion, but there are many more to chose from than those shown in this book if you want a different look.

The wadding (batting) should not be too firm or too smooth. I have usually used cotton wadding for the cushions, blankets and bags, but you could use polyester wadding if you want a higher loft. However, you could use anything from cotton wadding to stick-on felt, 2–4mm (1/16–1/8in) thick.

Many of the projects are strengthened with interfacing. I use the iron-on fusible types in the Vilene/Vlieseline range. In the project instructions, fusible interfacing means light- to medium-weight fusible interfacing to suit your fabric weight. A heavier weight, described as fusible pelmet interfacing, is needed to give body to some projects. A few projects call for double-sided fusible web, for which you could use Bondaweb/Vliesofix. Extraordinary or unusual materials are given in the instructions.

You can get the Tilda collection at Panduro Hobby and through their distributors.

www.tildasworld.com   www.pandurohobby.com

Angel Bodies

Patterns can be found on pages 138–139.

YOU WILL NEED:
Fabric for the skin
Fabric for the bodice
Fabric for the wings
Tilda hair or something similar
Embroidery yarn for the fringe
Wadding (batting)
A wooden pin or something similar for
turning right side out

INSTRUCTIONS:
These instructions are for the large angels
shown in different outfits throughout this book.
Instructions for the Cupcake Angel are on page 40.

The body parts are connected by a bodice, which
can be under a range of other garments, for
example a wraparound dress (page 83), a jacket
(page 36) or a skirt (page 35 or 92). Choose the
colour for the bodice to match the whole outfit.
Plain white fabric is a good solution if you are
not sure what to pick. Sew together the skin and
bodice fabrics (see Figure A). Then fold the whole
piece in half widthways, right sides together.

Fold the skin fabric for the legs and arms double.
Trace all of the pieces from the pattern (see
Figure A), and cut out. Cut notches in the seam
allowance where the seams curve inwards.

Turn the head and body right sides out. Turn the
legs and arms using the wooden pin. Press the
blunt end of the pin against the tip of the arm/leg
(see Figure B). Starting with the foot/hand, pull
the leg/arm down the wooden pin (see Figure C).
Pull the foot/hand at the same time as you hold
the leg/arm at the bottom so it will turn right
sides out (see Figure D).

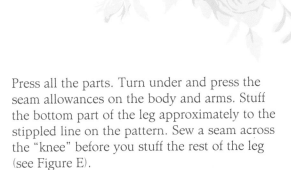

Press all the parts. Turn under and press the seam allowances on the body and arms. Stuff the bottom part of the leg approximately to the stippled line on the pattern. Sew a seam across the "knee" before you stuff the rest of the leg (see Figure E).

Stuff the head, body and arms. Place the legs inside the body and sew them on securely (see Figure F). Sew on the arms close to the body underneath the shoulder parts (see Figure G).

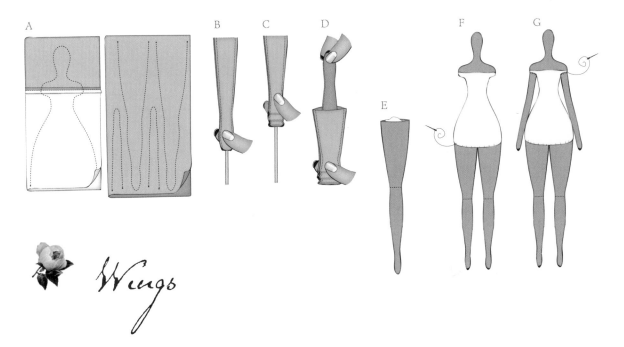

A   B   C   D   E   F   G

Wings

Fold the fabric for the wings double and trace the wings from the pattern. Sew around the wings (see Figure H). Turn right sides out and sew the stitched detail as shown in the pattern (see Figure I). Use the wooden pin to stuff the wings and sew together the opening.

Do not attach the wings to the angel before adding the clothes.

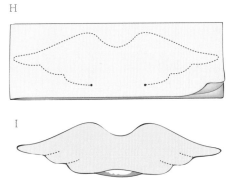

H

I

Hair

If you want, you can draw a line across the forehead with a vanishing ink pen or a thin pen in a pale colour to give a line to follow when you sew the fringe. Sew long close stitches to make the fringe, using embroidery yarn in a colour that matches the rest of the hair, and sew a few stitches a little longer down the cheek on each side (see Figure A).

Stick pins into the head, from the forehead down to the middle of the back of the head. Then stick another pin on each side of the head. Apply the hair from one side to the other, dividing it between the pins in the middle (see Figure B). When the head is completely covered, sew on the hair and remove the pins. Make two bundles of hair and attach one to each side of the head. Attach a rose with some glue (see Figure C).

If you are giving the angel a headscarf, as on page 55, it is a good idea not to have too much hair on each side of the head. That way the headscarf will look prettier. Attach the headscarf before adding the hair bundles.

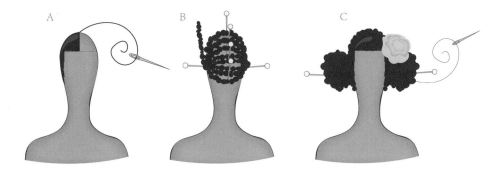

Face

On large angels and the Cupcake Angel you can use eye tools from the Tilda Face Painting set or small pinheads to make eyes.

Large pinheads are used on the giraffes, elephants and cockatoos.

Place two pins in the head to see where the eyes should be. Remove the pins. Dip the recommended tool or pinhead in black paint and stamp over the pin holes.
Apply Tilda blush from the Face Painting set or lipstick with a dry brush to make rosy cheeks.

The Studio

It's not easy to keep a studio tidy with everything that is supposed to be in there. My solution is to make different displays around the studio where I combine colours that look good together. That way the chaos looks a little nicer. In this display I chose green, turquoise and purple, which makes a lovely fresh combination.

 Embellishments

The cherry on the cake when sewing a bag, a hat or similar is the embellishment. Here are some pretty ideas for decorating your clothes and accessories.

The butterflies below make great hair accessories, and the flowers on page 19 can be used as brooches to attach to clothes or bags. The embroidered patches and yo-yos on page 21 will also add the perfect finishing touch to many of your projects.

 BUTTERFLIES

Pattern can be found on page 138.

YOU WILL NEED:
Fabric for the wings
Cotton wadding (batting), 3–4mm (¹⁄₁₆–¹⁄₈in) thick
Wooden pin, approximately 4mm (¹⁄₈in)
Embroidery yarn
Sequins, pearls and glitter glue

INSTRUCTIONS:
Fold fabric for the wings right sides together and place wadding (batting) underneath. Trace the wings from the pattern and sew around them. Cut out the butterfly wings and make an opening for turning through in one of the fabric layers. Turn right sides out and press the wings. Fold two small tucks and tack (baste) in place (see Figure A).

One end of the wooden pin should be sharp; you can easily sharpen it with a pencil sharpener. Cut the pin so it measures about 6cm (2³⁄₈in).

Tie the end of the embroidery yarn about 4mm (¹⁄₈in) from the sharp end of the pin. Twist the embroidery yarn around the pin, first down towards the sharp end, then upwards until the whole pin is covered (see Figure B).

Tack (baste) or glue the body to the middle of the wings. Sew on pearls and sequins and apply some glitter on the body.

You can either attach the butterfly to a jewellery pin or brooch so you can take it off whenever you want, or sew it directly onto the projects.

A

B

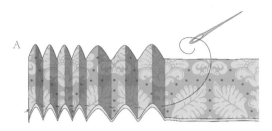

A

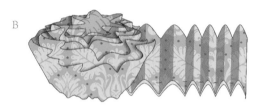

B

C

D

(1³⁄₈in) wide. Make small folds of approximately 1cm (³⁄₈in) and sew with embroidery yarn through all the folds (see Figure A). When the whole strip is done, roll and tack (baste) it loosely together. Finally, sew through all the layers to secure the flower (see Figure B).

ROSES

YOU WILL NEED:
Fabric
Embroidery yarn
A strong needle or something similar

INSTRUCTIONS:
Cut a strip 7cm (2³⁄₄in) wide. For the large roses use the whole width of the fabric. For the small roses use half the width of the fabric. A seam allowance is not necessary. Fold about 1cm (³⁄₈in) under on each side and fold the fabric strip double, wrong sides together, so it ends up being 3.5 cm (1³⁄₈in) wide.

Fold the top corner at the end of the strip downwards and twist the rest of the strip around it. The secret is to twist it loosely and fold the top edge of the strip down at regular intervals to create unevenness (see Figure C). Hold in place with pins while you are doing this.

At the end, sew through all the layers on the underside of the rose to secure.

CARNATION AND ROSE LEAVES

Patterns can be found on page 138.

The leaves come in two sizes, one for the large flower and one for the small.

Fold a piece of green fabric right sides together and trace the leaves from the pattern. Sew around the leaf, cut, turn it out and press. Tack (baste) together the opening and twist some thread around the middle of the leaf (see Figure D). Sew leaves to the underside of the flower.

CARNATIONS

YOU WILL NEED:
Fabric
Embroidery yarn
A strong needle or something similar

INSTRUCTIONS:
Cut a strip 7cm (2³⁄₄in) wide. For the large carnations use the whole fabric width and for the small carnations use half the fabric width. A seam allowance is not necessary. Fold in about 1cm (³⁄₈in) at each end. Then fold the fabric strip double, wrong sides together, so it will be 3.5cm

19

EMBROIDERED PATCHES

Embroidered patches were used to cover up holes in trousers when I was a little girl, but they are also nice to use as embellishments and I have used them on several projects in this book. They come in various styles in the Tilda collection.

YO-YOS

I used a yo-yo on the small beauty bag pictured below and the appliqué cushion on page 105.

You make the yo-yo by cutting a circle of fabric twice the size of the finished yo-yo, plus seam allowance. Fold in the seam allowance, tack (baste) along the edge, gather it together and secure the thread.

A small pompom trim is sewn around the edge on the reverse of the yo-yo before it is sewn to the beauty bag, so only the pompoms show. Pearls and buttons are also sewn on to embellish the bag.

 *Bracelet*

Pattern can be found on page 140.

A

YOU WILL NEED:
Fabric
Fusible pelmet interfacing
A small decorative fastening or similar
Embellishments (textile brads, pearls and sequins)

INSTRUCTIONS:
Trace the bracelet from the pattern onto strong vliselin and onto your desired fabric. Be aware when you decide how to place the pattern on the fabric that the bracelet will be folded. Cut out the piece in fusible pelmet interfacing without a seam allowance and add more than enough seam allowance when you cut out the fabric piece. Iron the fabric piece to the adhesive side of the interfacing. Turn the bracelet over and press the seam allowance (see Figure A).

Fold the bracelet in half lengthways and press so you get a clear visible fold.

If you want to attach textile brads, use sharp scissors to make small holes through the bracelet. Push the metal legs of the textile brads through the holes and fold them out on the reverse. Sew on pearls and sequins if desired.

Sew together the open sides of the bracelet (see Figure B).

Attach the decorative fastening to open and close the bracelet (see Figure C).

B

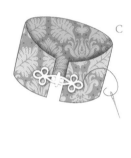

C

Rings

YOU WILL NEED:
Fabric
Fusible pelmet interfacing
Double-sided fusible web
Embellishments (pearls and sequins)

INSTRUCTIONS:
Cut out a small strip of fusible pelmet interfacing, 1.5cm (⅝in) wide and about 8cm (3¼in) long.

Use the strip to measure around your finger so it fits and is not too tight. Iron double-sided fusible web to the wrong side of a fabric and cut out a strip that is 4cm (1⅜in) wide and 1.5cm (⅝in) wider than the strip of interfacing. Place the strip of interfacing against the wrong side of the fabric strip and cut the corners of the fabric strip (see Figure D). Fold in the edges and press to bond (see Figure E).

Sew together the ends of the strip to make it into a ring (see Figure F). Sew on pearls or sequins.

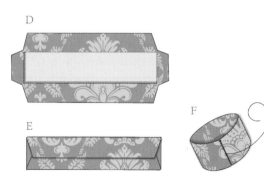

D

E

F

Belts

Pattern can be found on page 140.

YOU WILL NEED:
Fabric for the belt, ribbon and flower
Fusible pelmet interfacing
Double-sided fusible web
Embroidered patch or embellishments

INSTRUCTIONS:
The belt pattern is divided in two parts to fit
the pattern page. Put the two parts together,
matching points A and B.

Also, the pattern is marked with folding edges in
two directions. Trace the pattern four times onto
the fusible pelmet interfacing, rotating each time
to create a large oval shape (see Figure A).

Cut out the interfacing belt shape without a seam
allowance. Then cut out the same shape in fabric,
but add 1cm (⅜in) seam allowance around the
edge. Bond the fabric to the interfacing shape
using double-sided fusible web. Fold and press
the seam allowance along the edge. Fold the belt
in half lengthways and press (see Figure B).

Cut two strips that measure 8cm (3¼in) wide,
using the whole fabric width. Iron in one of the
ends and approximately 1.5cm (⅝in) along the
long sides. Fold the strip twice so it is about
2.5cm (1in) wide and sew together the open long
sides and the folded short end on each strip (see
Figure C).

Attach the strips to each side of the belt with a
large pin and try on the belt. Let the strips cross
at the back and tie a bow in front on your right
side (see picture). If the strips are too long you can
place a pin where you want them to end. Then cut
each strip at the end that is not yet sewn.

Tack (baste) each strip on the open ends of the
belt and sew around the ends to attach (see
Figure D).

The flower is made of a strip of fabic, 2cm x
60cm (¾in x 32in). Place the short ends right
sides together and sew. Fold the strip in half
lengthways, wrongs sides together, so it is
6cm (2⅜in) wide. Sew along the open side
with embroidery yarn and gather up. Attach
an embroidered patch (see page 21) or other
embellishment to the middle and sew the flower
to the belt on the opposite side of where you tie
the bow (see picture).

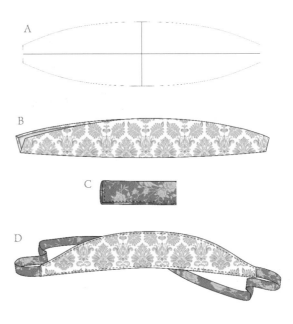

Laptop Case

Patterns can be found on page 143.

YOU WILL NEED:
Fusible pelmet interfacing
Double-sided fusible web
Fabric for the case
Fabric for the lining
A decorative fastening
Embroidered patch or embellishments

INSTRUCTIONS:
The pattern is only for the case cover since laptops come in different sizes. The pattern is made for a 37.5cm (15in) laptop and can be adjusted slightly to suit other sizes.

The pattern is divided in two parts. Place the parts together to match points A and B. The pattern gives half the shape of the flap.

Take a tape measure to measure around your laptop (see Figure A) and add 4cm (1⅝in). Measure the width and depth of the laptop (see Figure B) and add 3cm (1¼in).

Draw a rectangle on the fusible pelmet interfacing using these measurements, making sure there is enough room for the flap at one end.

Place the pattern for the flap along the top of the rectangle, matching the corner, and trace the pattern. Repeat the same procedure on the opposite side (see Figure C). It doesn't matter if the flap patterns don't touch each other or if they overlap by a small amount. However, if there is a significant gap, the pattern should be resized with a photocopier.

Cut out the whole case in fabric. Bond the fabric to the interfacing and cut around the shape. Then bond the double-sided fusible web to the wrong side of the lining and pull off the paper. Protect the ironing board with baking paper or scrap fabric. Place the adhesive side of the lining on the side with the interfacing of the case, and bond the lining to the case. Cut around the edge.

Fold over the extra 4cm (1⅝in) of fabric along the bottom edge so it covers the raw edge of the lining. Press and sew this border down. Fold the bottom part of the case upwards so it meets the base of the flap. You can use the pattern to measure if you want. Press the fold.

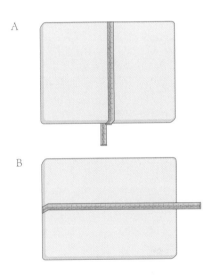

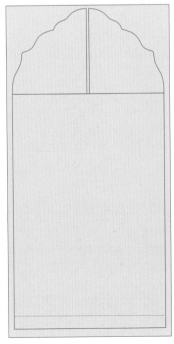

27

Use a pair of scissors to round the bottom corners (see Figure D).

Pin the two parts of the case together and sew a close 6mm (¼in) zigzag stitch around the whole purse (see Figure E).

Attach an embroidered patch on the flap. Place the laptop in the case to position the decorative fastening and then sew it in place.

CARRYING STRAP

You can see a mobile phone case with a carrying strap on page 81.

Cut a strip of fusible pelmet interfacing measuring 4.5cm x 50 cm (1¾in x 20in), and a fabric strip measuring 7cm x 50 cm (2¾in x 20in). Bond the interfacing to the wrong side of the fabric strip. Press the fabric edges over the interfacing before you fold the strip in half lengthways. Sew along the open side (see Figure F).

Make sure you sew the strip securely to the purse (see Figure G).

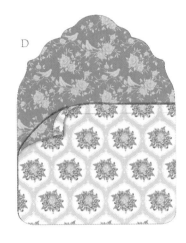

D

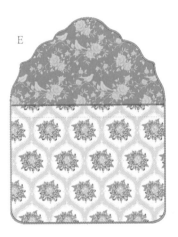

E

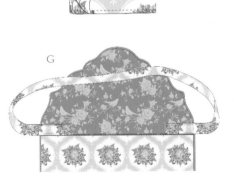

F

G

 *Hats*

Pattern can be found on page 143.

YOU WILL NEED:
Wool felt
Fabric for the border
Embellishments (see page 16)

INSTRUCTIONS:
The pattern is divided in two parts. Place the two parts together to match points A and B.

Fold and iron the wool felt right sides together and trace the hat pattern. Sew around the top edges (see Figure A). Cut out the hat, taking care along the drawn line around the opening of the hat. Turn right sides out.

Cut a strip of fabric measuring 5cm x 110 cm (2in x 45in) and press it in half lengthways so it is 2.5cm (1in) wide. Place the open side of the strip around the open edge of the hat, matching the edges and right sides together. Sew 6mm (¼in) from the edge (see Figure B).

Fold the strip around the edge of the hat and sew it to the inside.

The flowers and butterflies from pages 16–19 could be added as embellishments.

A

B

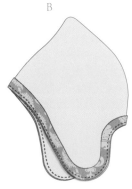

Bulletin Board

YOU WILL NEED:
Base for the bulletin board, see below
Thick wadding (batting)
Fabric for the board
Fabric strips
Various ribbons
Staple gun

INSTRUCTIONS:
You can use a canvas stretcher for the bulletin board, or as I have done here, use an insulation board. You can easily cut it to the desired size with a craft knife.

Cut out a piece of fabric and a piece of wadding (batting) big enough to cover the front side of the board and be attached to the reverse. Tighten the fabric and wadding (batting) around the board and staple them to the reverse with a staple gun.

Fabric strips can be used in addition to ribbons. Cut the strips twice as wide as you want the finished strip to be and iron in the sides so they meet in the middle (see Figure A).

Tighten fabric strips (wrong side on the board) and ribbons around the board and attach them to the reverse (see Figure B).

The reverse will not be visible when the board is hanging on a wall or standing against a wall, but if you are neat you could attach a backing fabric. Cut the fabric a little bigger than the board and press the edges under so the backing is a bit smaller than the board. Slipstitch the edge to the fabric on the reverse of the board (see Figure C).

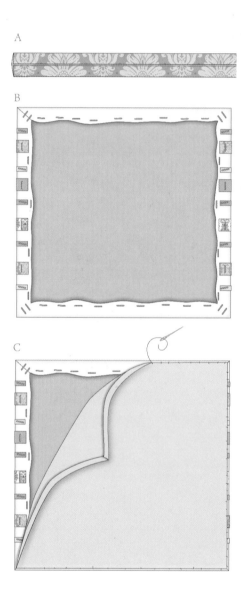

A

B

C

Studio Angel

YOU WILL NEED:
Materials for the angel, see page 10
Fabric for the skirt
Fabric for the pantaloons
Ribbon to embellish
Paper flower

INSTRUCTIONS:
Sew the angel as described on pages 10–11.

PANTALOONS

Pattern can be found on page 142.

Use the pattern to cut out four pantaloon parts, adding enough seam allowance along the top of the waist and for the leg hems. Place two matching parts right sides together and sew as shown in Figure A. Repeat with the other two parts and press.

Place the parts right sides together and sew the seams as shown in Figure B.

Fold the pantaloons so the seams lie over each other and sew the inside leg seams (see Figure C).

SKIRT

Cut a piece of fabric measuring 54cm x 20cm (22in x 8in) for the skirt and add a seam allowance. Fold the skirt right sides together widthways so it is 27cm x 20cm (11in x 8in). Sew the open sides closed. Turn right side out. Turn up a hem at the bottom and turn under the seam allowance at the top. Press.

You can sew on ribbons at the bottom edge if desired.

Pin the skirt around the angel's waist. Make two tucks in front and two tucks in the back of the waist. Attach the skirt with tacking stitches (see Figure D).

BODICE

Fold in the edges of a strip of fabric and attach it around the shoulders. Sew it to the back before you attach the wings.

D

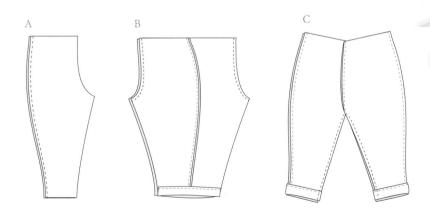

A   B   C

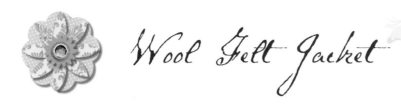

Wool Felt Jacket

Pattern can be found on page 141.

YOU WILL NEED:
Wool felt
Mini pompom trim
A decorative fastening

INSTRUCTIONS:
Cut out a left and right jacket front, one back piece and one collar using the pattern. Note that you do not need a seam allowance along the dotted lines.

Place the front and back parts right sides together and sew as shown in Figure A. Place the right side of the collar against the wrong side of the jacket, and sew a seam close to the edge. You could also use a zigzag stitch to sew even closer to the edge (see Figure B).

The collar seam is supposed to face outwards, but will be covered by the collar at the end.

Turn out and press the jacket carefully. You could sew a pompom trim along the edge of the whole jacket (see picture opposite). Dress the angel with the jacket and pin the decorative fastening to check that it is correctly positioned before you attach it. The jacket could be decorated with a paper flower or similar if desired.

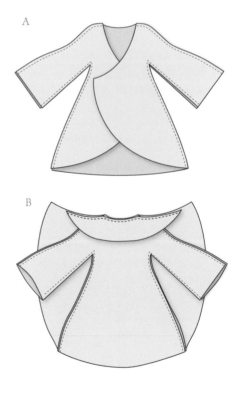

A

B

Grandma's China

I inherited a set of blue and white china for 40 people from my grandma. I usually don't have that many guests, but I really love the china. This chapter is inspired by my grandma's china and the combination of old and new. You will find cupcake angels and some ideas for table arrangements.

Cupcake Angel

Cupcakes are so delicious - one more, then just one more... and before you know it you will feel like one of these angels! Suddenly it's hard to fly. Cupcake Angels look cute in the Bird Cage on page 65.

Patterns can be found on pages 144-145.

YOU WILL NEED:
Fabric for the skin
Fabric for the wings
Tilda hair or similar
Embroidery yarn for the fringe
Wool felt for the dress
Fabric for the gathered trim
Ribbon to embellish
3mm pearl beads for the buttons
Wadding (batting)
A wooden pin or similar for turning right side out

INSTRUCTIONS:
Fold the skin fabric right sides together and trace the angel from the pattern. Sew as shown in Figure A. Cut out the angel and close the openings on each side of the stomach, as shown in Figure B. Make an opening for turning through one of the layers, turn out and iron the angel. The opening will be hidden by the dress at the end. Use the wooden pin to stuff the arms and legs, and then stuff the whole angel. Sew the opening closed.

Fold the wool felt right sides together. Trace the dress from the pattern and then sew around it (see Figure C).

Cut out the dress and note that the openings are marked with a dotted line and should be cut on the pattern line. Allow small seam allowances along the other edges. Sew the seams and cut out the dress. Turn right side out and iron the dress carefully.

A   B   C

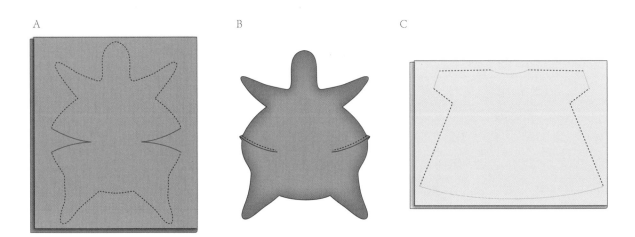

Cut a strip of fabric measuring 75cm x 7cm (30in x 2¾in), seam allowance included. Iron the strip in half lengthways so it is 75cm x 3.5cm (30in x 1⅜in). Sew along the long open side with large running stitches through both layers. Gather the strip until it is the same length as the bottom edge of the dress, plus a seam allowance. Starting at the back in the middle of the dress, place the border underneath the edge of the dress and sew it on with a zigzag stitch (see Figure D).

Sew the ends of the strip together at the back. Sew on a ribbon to cover up the join between the dress and the pleated border.

Dress the angel and make the hair and face as described on page 13.

Cut out the collar and attach it around the angel's neck with a few stitches in the front (see Figure E). Fold down the collar. Sew on three pearls as buttons.

The Cupcake Angels have two separate wings instead of one big wing as for the large angels.

Fold the fabric for the wings double and trace the two wings from the pattern. Sew around, but don't close the opening for turning. Cut out, turn right side out and iron the wings. Sew stitch lines as marked in the pattern, and stuff the same way as for the double wings on page 11. Close the opening and sew on the wings so they are visible from the front (see picture below). You could also attach a ribbon to the back as a hanger.

D

E

Pleasant Company

You may have found your place on this earth with a few good friends who are interesting because you have common interests or maybe because you are so different.
You might want to show that you appreciate them or, on other occasions, new acquaintances. Either way, it's always nice to show your appreciation. Always bring a little something for your hostess or, if you are hosting yourself, make an extra nice party. Here we decorated a very feminine tea table with a lot of decorative elements.

Party Decorations

To make cute cards with colourful angels, attach the angels to the card using double-sided adhesive tabs and apply some glitter.

Fabric flowers from page 19 are nice for the hair and as decorations for the table.

Piles of cups, bowls and plates are used at your own risk and should be removed before the liqueur is brought to the table! It may be better to use inexpensive china from a flea market for this purpose...

Pretty in Pink

Colours bring energy and joy. They are more flamboyant than neutral colours and that may be the reason why people are often afraid to use too much of them. I always try to challenge myself with new colours, and often I find new and interesting combinations in the process. Here I put together red, cerise and pink with elements of turquoise, orange and green.

Colourful Details

The roses from page 19 are used as embellishments on shoes and on a simple white dress. The bracelets from page 22 look good in red and pink. You can find the bird cage on page 65, here in red with pompom trim. New cushions can be an easy way to make some changes in your home and you can find fabric bowls on page 60.

Summer Angel

Pattern can be found on page 144.

YOU WILL NEED:
Materials for the angel (see page 10)
Fabric for the skirt and pleated trim
Fabric for the headscarf
Pompom trim, if desired

INSTRUCTIONS:
Sew the angel as described on page 10.

PLEATED TRIM AND SKIRT

Cut a strip of fabric that measures 3cm x 40cm
(1¼in x 16in) for the pleated trim and a strip of
approximately 10cm x 40cm (4in x 16in) for the
skirt. Add more than enough seam allowance
to all sides.

Turn and press the seam allowances along the
long edges of both strips. Sew pompom trim
along the bottom edge of the skirt if desired.

Fold the skirt strip right sides together and sew
the shortest sides together (see Figure A).

Sew together the short sides of the pleated trim
in the same way.

Pin the trim around the shoulders in pleats and
then sew it in place (see Figure B).

Arrange the skirt around the hips in pleats and
sew (see Figure C).

A
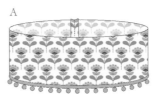

B
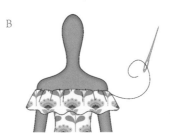

C

HEADSCARF

Fold the fabric for the headscarf right sides together
and trace the shape from the pattern. Sew around the
shape, cut and turn it out. Press.

Sew the hair as described on page 13 without
attaching the hair bundles.

Use pins to attach the headscarf tightly around the
head, crossing it over at the back without tying it. Sew
it firmly (see Figure D).

Pin the hair bundles on each side of the head and sew
them on (see Figure E).

Make the face of the angel as described on page 13.

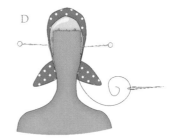

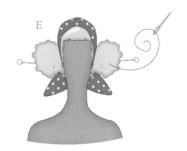

Cherries

Pattern can be found on page 144.

Fold the fabric for the cherries and leaves double and trace two cherries and one pair of leaves from the pattern. Sew around the shapes (see Figure A).

Cut out the shapes, turn right sides out and press.

Cut two lengths of thin metal wire measuring approximately 25cm (10in) and twist them together until you have 5cm (2in) in from each end that is not twisted. Fold the twisted wire as shown in Figure B. Twist the folded end so you get a small loop (see Figure C).

Press in the seam allowance around the opening of the cherries and tack (baste) around it. Stuff them with wadding (batting) and place the ends of the wire inside (see Figure D). Gather up the opening and secure.

Tie the leaves around the stalk just underneath the loop (see Figure E).

The cherries are a nice accessory for the angel on page 53 and can be sewn on to one of the hands (see Figure F).

Little Cherry Ideas

Cards and patches with cherry motifs are great for gifts from the kitchen. With the help of a hole punch you can make holes in the cards and thread them on ribbons as I have done here.

You can find the pattern for the little cards on page 144.

Fabric Bowls

Pattern can be found on page 145.

YOU WILL NEED:
Fusible pelmet interfacing
Double-sided fusible web
Fabric for the outside
Fabric for the inside

INSTRUCTIONS:
The bowl comes in two different pattern sizes. Note that the larger pattern is marked with a fold and needs to be cut from a double layer of fabric.

Trace the bowl and bottom onto fusible pelmet interfacing and cut out the parts. Bond the outside fabric to the interfacing parts and cut around. Then bond double-sided fusible web to the wrong side of the lining and pull off the paper. Protect the ironing board with baking paper or some scrap fabric. Place the adhesive side of the lining down onto the interfaced side of the bowl parts and iron. Cut around the edges.

Sew the bowl sides to the bottom with a close 6mm (¼in) zigzag stitch without the edges overlapping each other (see Figure A).

Sew the two open edges together in a similar way to complete the bowl shape (see Figure B).

Finally, sew a close 4mm (⅛in) zigzag stitch around the edge of the bowl.

The bowl can be turned inside out if you want the lining side outwards.

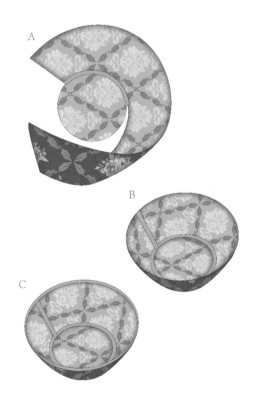

Inspired by Birds

Birds are often a source of inspiration for me – especially my cockatoo Kikko, who keeps me company in place of colleagues. He talks, sings, dances and creates a nice atmosphere. Here he is the centre of attention and poses as a model for the first time. This chapter is for bird lovers, but you will also find a lot of other ideas.

Bird Cage

Patterns can be found on pages 146–147.

YOU WILL NEED:
Fusible pelmet interfacing
Fabric for the cage
Fabric for the cage mat
Wadding (batting), 3–4mm (¹⁄₁₆in–¹⁄₈in) thick
Steel wire

INSTRUCTIONS:
Use a cutting mat, a rotary cutter and a patchwork ruler to cut the fabric.

For the cage ribs, cut ten strips of fusible pelmet interfacing measuring 36cm x 1cm (14¹⁄₈in x ³⁄₈in) and one strip measuring 72cm x 1cm (28¹⁄₄in x ³⁄₈in) Cut another strip measuring 72cm x 8cm (28¹⁄₄in x 3¹⁄₄in) for the cage base. Cut thin wire the same lengths as the ribs (see Figure A).

Cut ten fabric strips that measure 36cm x 3.5cm (14¹⁄₈in x 1³⁄₈in) for the short ribs and one fabric strip of 74cm x 3.5cm (29in x 1³⁄₈in) for the long rib. Seam allowances are included.

Start by sewing the wire onto the adhesive side of the interfaced ribs with a zigzag stitch (see Figure B).

Bond the ribs to the wrong side of the fabric so the wire lies down on the fabric and approximately 7mm (³⁄₈in) from the edge (see Figure C). The fabric is supposed to be 1cm (³⁄₈in) longer than the longest rib at each end.

Turn and press the seam allowance on each long side of the fabric strip (see Figure D). Fold the fabric over again and sew along the long open side (see Figure E).

Cut and sew two wires to the wide strip for the base on the side without adhesive. Place one about 1cm (³⁄₈in) down from the edge and the other about 3cm (1¹⁄₄in) down (see Figure F).

Cut out a fabric strip of 74cm x 10cm (29in x 4in), and bond it to the adhesive side of the interfacing. Fold over the seam allowances and fold the strip in half lengthways so it is 4cm (1⁵⁄₈in) wide (see Figure G). Do not close the strip.

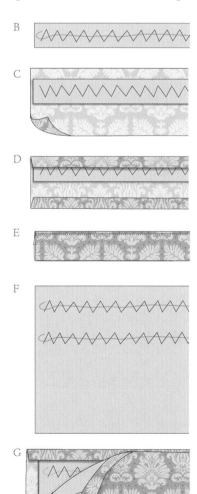

A

B

C

D

E

F

G

Starting 1cm (⅜in) in from the end of the base strip, place the ribs in between the layers, leaving approximately 7cm (2¾in) gaps. The ribs should lie on the fold of the strip. Attach the ribs with pins (see Figure H).

Sew together the open side of the base, securing the ribs. Be careful when you sew across pins and wire. Measure 15cm (6in) and place the long rib across the short ones. Make sure that the ribs remain evenly spaced. Attach the cross rib with pins and stitch along each long side (see Figure I).

Make a circle of the bird cage and fold the fabric seam allowancein at one end and out at the other end of the base and cross rib (see Figure J). The

edges should overlap each other by 1cm (⅜in), so the circumference of the bird cage will be 70cm (27½in). Sew the ends together.
Fold fabric for the two circles right sides together and place a piece of wadding (batting) underneath. Trace the circles from the pattern. Sew around and cut out the circles. Make an opening on each one, through one layer, and then turn out and press the circles. Sew the openings closed.

Sew all the ribs to the smaller circle about 1cm (⅜in) from the edge. The opening on the circle should face upwards. Cut a slightly smaller circle in interfacing, and place it over the first circle with the adhesive side down.

H

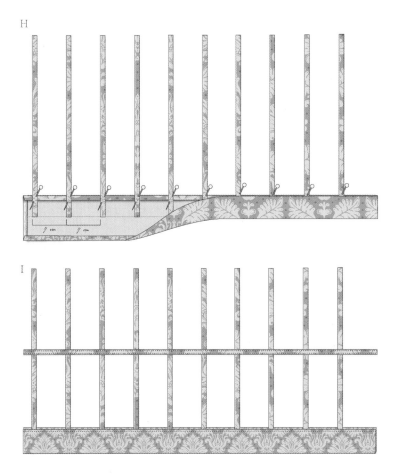

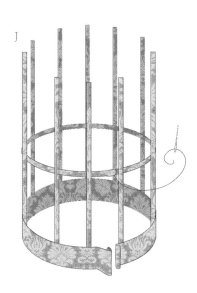

Place a folded piece of fabric or similar underneath and bond the circles together (see Figure K). Place the larger fabric circle on top with the opening downwards and sew it to the other circle around the edge (see Figure L).

Note that the pattern for the cage bottom should be cut on the fold.

Cut out a piece of interfacing, a piece of fabric and a piece of lining to fit the cage bottom. Bond the lining to the interfacing and place the fabric right sides together on top. Trace and sew around the cage bottom, leaving an opening about 12cm (5in) long in the seam.

Cut and turn out the circle. Use a wooden stick or similar to push out the edges. Fold in the edges around the opening and sew them together. The pattern for the bottom can be placed on top so you can see that the shape is correct as you sew.

Sew the bottom edge to the underside of the bird cage, so the lining is facing into the bird cage (see Figure M).

Sew on a ribbon to the top as a hanger if desired.

K

L

M
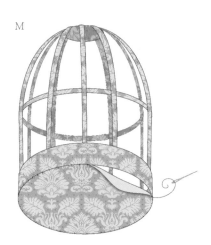

Cockatoos

Pattern can be found on page 147.

YOU WILL NEED:
Fabric for the body
Fabric for the bill
Wooden stand
Toy stuffing
Embellishments, if desired

INSTRUCTIONS:
The cockatoo pattern is divided in two parts to fit the pattern page. Place the two parts together to match points A and B.

Trace two reversed pieces for the body and cut them out with more than enough seam allowance. Cut a precise 6mm (¹/₄in) seam allowance along the bill seam.

Trace and cut out two reversed bill parts, again with more than enough seam allowance, but precisely 6 mm along the body seam (see Figure A). The curve on the bill could be difficult to make so it's a good idea to sew it on by hand. Place the bill/body seam edge by edge and sew along the line (see Figure B). Press the bill open.

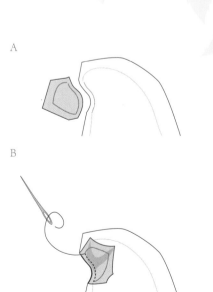

A

B

Place the two body parts right sides together and sew around the body and bill (see Figure C).

Cut and turn out the body. Stuff the body and sew the opening closed (see Figure D). Use a wooden stick or similar to push out the tail and sew under the belly so you will get a nice curve (see Figure E).

Fold fabric for the wings right sides together and trace a left and right wing. Sew around and cut out. Make an opening through the inside of each wing so they are both facing inwards when you sew the wings onto the bird. Turn out and press the wings.

Sew lines on the wings as marked on the pattern (see Figure F). Use a wooden stick or similar to stuff between the seams, and then stuff the rest of the wings thoroughly. Use an iron to flatten out the wings. Then sew them to the body with the opening inwards.

Make the cockatoo's face as described on page 13. Sharpen the tip of the stick on the wooden stand and twist it into the bird. If you want, you can attach a paper flower or some ribbon onto the cockatoo to embellish.

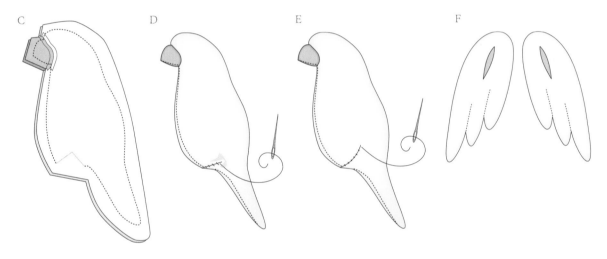

Iron-on Décor

Motifs can be found on pages 136 and 137.

YOU WILL NEED:
Transfer paper to work with your fabric
Scanner/printer or photocopier
Craft knife
Something to iron on

INSTRUCTIONS:
The motifs can either be scanned or printed out onto transfer paper, or photocopied. Follow the manufacturer's instructions.

I'm sure there are a lot of different types of transfer paper, with different instructions, but here are a few tips.

It is okay to cut out the motif precisely, but it's a good idea to leave a little bit of the background. It can be a challenge to peel the covering from the paper, so it's good to have a little bit of background so you don't damage the motif. Use a craft knife to divide the covering from the paper.

Cut away the extra background after you have peeled off the covering, so the motif is correct.

Beyond that, follow the instructions on the packaging, but be careful with the temperature of the iron when you attach the motif to the fabric. Try out a few samples first, as the heat could make the motif shrink or turn yellow.

3D Iron-on Décor

Motifs can be found on pages 136 and 137.

YOU WILL NEED:
Iron-on motifs
White fabric
Disappearing ink pen
Toy stuffing
String as a hanger

INSTRUCTIONS:
Iron the motif to the white fabric as described on page 73. Place the fabric on a window pane or bright surface with the motif facing down so you can see traces of it through the fabric. Draw a contour about 1cm (⅜in) outside the motif with the disappearing ink pen. Remember that you are supposed to sew on the line, so the shapes should be quite easy (see illustration).

Place a piece of fabric underneath the motif fabric, right sides together. Then sew along the drawn line.

On simple shapes like the bird cage you could have the turning opening in the seam, but on more complicated shapes the opening should be cut through the back layer of the fabric.

Cut out the motif and use a wooden stick or similar to turn out the shape.

Stuff the shape and sew the opening closed. The opening will look prettier if you sew a small patch over it. Fold under the raw edges on a small piece of fabric and sew it on over the opening.

If the motif loosens during the process, place the ironing paper (which comes with the transfer paper) over it and bond it more.

Decorate the motif with glitter glue if desired.

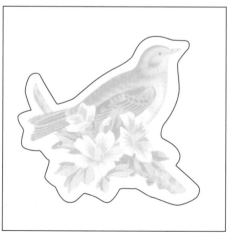

Large Bag

YOU WILL NEED:
Fabric for the bag
Fabric for the lining
Fabric for the borders
Cotton wadding (batting)
Zipper, 50cm (20in)

INSTRUCTIONS:
Adding more than enough seam allowance to all the parts, cut two pieces of fabric, two pieces of lining and two pieces of wadding (batting), 50cm (20in) from top to bottom, 80cm (32in) wide across the bottom with sides narrowing towards the top, 50cm (20in) across the top (see Figure A).

Place one piece of lining, right side down, over the wrong side of the zipper, matching the edges. Sew the lining to the zipper (see Figure B).

Fold the lining back so the zipper is visible, and sew the other piece of lining to the other side of the zipper the same way (see Figure C).

A

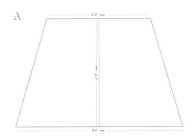

B

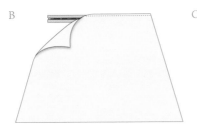

C

Place the fabric wrong side down on the wadding (batting) and pin the layers together. Then attach these pieces to the right side of the zipper (see Figure D).

Fold the fabric and lining away from the zipper on top of each other as shown in Figure E. If you wish, you can quilt the bag.

Remove any pins and fold the bag right sides together. Close the bottom of the bag with zigzag stitch.

Cut a strip that measures 80cm x 5cm (32in x 2in) in the lining fabric. Press the strip in half lengthways so it is 80cm x 2.5cm (32in x 1in). Place the open side against the bottom edge of the bag and sew about 7mm (³/₈in) in (see Figure F).

Fold the strip over the edge and sew it to the other side.

Turn out the bag. Measure 11cm (4¹/₄in) from the bottom and fold the bottom up into the bag (see Figure G). Cut the edges of the bag so they are even and also cut away the triangles sticking out at the bottom.

Sew along the sides with zigzag stitch to keep the layers together.

Cut strips of fabric as long as the sides of the bag plus 2cm (³/₄in), and 5cm (2in) wide.

Press the strip in half lengthways and attach them to the sides in the same way as the bottom, folding in the extra allowance at the top and bottom first. This way you hide the raw edges.

CARRYING STRAP

Cut a strip measuring 8cm x 60 cm (3¹/₄in x 24in), and a strip of wadding (batting) measuring 6cm x 58cm (2³/₈in x 23in). Place the wadding (batting) centrally on the wrong side of the fabric. Turn over the fabric seam allowance along the long sides and press. Press the strip in half lengthways. Sew along the open long side.

To make the strap prettier, you can sew an additional line of stitches along the folded long side.

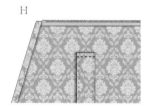

Measure 12cm (4³/₄in) towards the centre from each side of the bag and 5cm (2in) down from the zipper. Attach the ends securely to the bag as shown in Figures H and I.

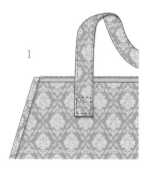

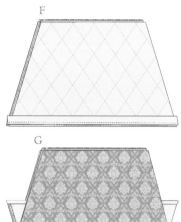

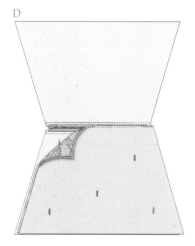

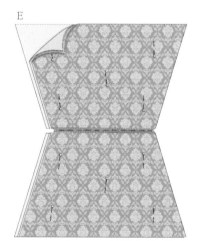

Mobile Phone Case

Pattern can be found on page 146.

YOU WILL NEED:
Fabric for the case
Fabric for the lining
Fusible pelmet interfacing
Double-sided fusible web

INSTRUCTIONS:
This case is designed to fit iPhones and other phones of a similar size. You can reduce the size of the pattern with the help of a photocopier if your mobile phone is smaller.

Cut one piece of fabric from the whole pattern and one piece from the lower part up to the dotted line. Only add 1cm (³⁄₈in) seam allowance above the dotted line on the smaller piece, and cut the rest on the pattern line. Bond the fabric and lining to the fusible pelmet interfacing the same way as for the laptop case on page 27.

Fold and sew the seam allowance down on the smaller part (see Figure A).

Cut a strip of interfacing 5mm (¹⁄₄in) wider than the case and a fabric strip just as long and 5cm (2in) deep. Bond the adhesive side of the strip to the wrong side of the fabric approximately 1cm (³⁄₈in) from the edge. Fold 1cm (³⁄₈in) in on each side of the fabric strip (see Figure B).

Fold the fabric side over the interfaced side and sew them together.

Place the lining side of the front pocket down against the lining side of the main case. Place the strip about 1cm (³⁄₈in) down from the top edge of the pocket. Attach the strip with pins so it lies edge to edge on each side. Sew around the whole case with a close 4mm (¹⁄₈in) zigzag stitch (see Figure C).

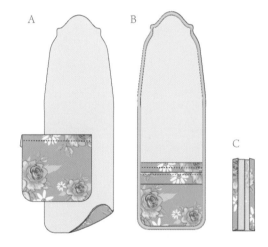

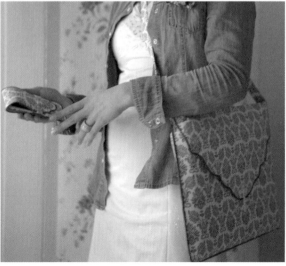

Blue Angels

Pattern can be found on pages 146-147.

YOU WILL NEED:
Angels (see page 10)
Fabric for the dress
Fabric for the pantaloons
Ribbons

INSTRUCTIONS:
Sew the angel as described on page 10. Make the hair and face as described on page 13. Sew the pantaloons as described on page 35.

WRAPAROUND DRESS

These instructions are for the dress and ribbon, but you could replace the ribbon with a button or textile brad if preferred.

The dress pattern is divided into two parts. Place the two pieces together, matching points A and B. The back piece should be cut on the fold.

83

The dress consists of three parts: one back piece and two front pieces, which follow the dotted line. Remember to cut a left and right front piece. Add seam allowances to all the parts when you cut them and a little extra allowance to hem the sleeves and bottom of the dress.

Cut two pieces of ribbon measuring 15cm (6in).

Place the front pieces of the dress right sides together on the back piece. Place one of the ribbons between the layers so it will be attached about 2cm (¾in) below the armpits. Sew the shoulder and side seams as shown in Figure A.

Turn under and press the seam allowance along the front edges and neckline. Turn the dress right side out. Sew the seam allowance around the front edges and neckline, attaching the other ribbon as shown in Figure B.

Fold in, press and sew the seam allowance to hem the sleeves and bottom of the dress. Sew ribbon along the bottom edge of the dress if desired (see picture on page 82).

Paper Bird Cage

YOU WILL NEED:
Patterned card
Metal tubes for tea lights
Thin steel wire
Tilda bird
Pearl bead
Ribbon for a hanger
Strong paper adhesive
Craft knife, ruler and cutting mat

INSTRUCTIONS:
Cut a rectangle of card 17.5cm x 12cm (7 x 4¾in). Place the right side face down on the cutting mat. Scratch a line across the top and bottom of the paper, 1.5cm (⅝in) from the edge. Then mark lines every 5mm (¼in) between the two scratched lines. Cut the lines through the paper (see Figure A). It is very important that you cut all the way through the paper, so cut twice if you don't get through the first time.

Glue the two outside ribs together to make a cylinder (see Figure B). Cut two strips of paper big enough to be glued around the two metal tubes and glue them in place. Make a central hole through the bottom of each tube.

Cut a long piece of wire and make a loop at one end. Use a strong needle or similar to make a hole in the bird. Thread the wire through the tube top, then through the paper cylinder, then through the bird, and last through the bottom tube. Thread a pearl bead on to the wire (see Figure D). Pull the wire. Help to wriggle the bird into the cylinder by turning its face up and its tail down. Pull until the cage has a nice round shape (see Figure D). Secure the wire by twisting it around the pearl bead and then cut away the rest.

Attach string to the loop as a hanger.

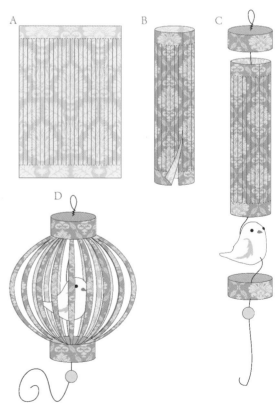

Bird Décor

Bird motifs are beautiful and suit with any occasion. It doesn't have to be complicated – one motif or a detail is often enough. You could decorate the motif with some glitter and a nice ribbon.

You can get finished bird découpage motifs at craft stores and use them to decorate gift boxes and cards. The layers are built out with double-sided adhesive pads, which creates an attractive 3D effect.

The pattern for gift cards can be found on page 144.

Green Inspiration

I was inspired to write this chapter by living 'green' and going to flea markets, but also by the colour green. A little bit of purple and turquoise are also used to break up the green. In this chapter you will find ideas for blankets and fabric water lilies, among many others.

Pink Angel

YOU WILL NEED:
Materials for the angel (see page 10)
3 different fabrics for the skirt
Fabric for the sash
Embroidery yarn

INSTRUCTIONS:
Make the angel as described on page 10, make face and hair as described on page 13 and trim the bodice as described on page 35.

Cut a strip of fabric measuring 10cm x 80 cm (4in x 32in), another one measuring 10cm x 65cm (4in x 26in) and one measuring 10cm x 50cm (4in x 20in), adding seam allowances.

Turn and press the seam allowance. Sew the allowance along the bottom long edge on the longest strip. Sew a gathering stitch along the upper long edge.

Gather the fabric until it is the same length as the next longest strip. Place the two strips right sides together and sew (see Figure A). Then gather the remaining long side of the middle strip until it is the same length as the shortest strip. Attach it to the shortest strip in the same way.

Fold the skirt right sides together widthways and sew the open sides together. Press under the seam allowance around the top of the skirt. Sew the top edge of the skirt to the angel with embroidery yarn. The waist of the skirt is supposed to be placed between the waistline and hips.

Tear a strip of fabric measuring 10cm x 80cm (4in x 32in). Then make the corners rounder. Tie the strip around the top of the skirt. If desired, you can attach a sewn rose (see page 19) over the knot.

A

Living Room in Green

An angel is sitting dreaming away in green surroundings. The table is decorated with water lilies from page 96, and the angel from page 10 is wearing the wraparound dress from page 83. This angel's dress has a ribbon in the same fabric and a contrasting fringe at the bottom.

RIBBONS AND FRINGE

You can make the ribbon for the dress by cutting two strips in the dress fabric of approximately 3cm x 15cm (1¼in x 6in). There is no need to add seam allowances. Fold and press about 6mm (¼in) along each long side before you fold the strip in half lengthways and press. Sew along the open edge. The ribbons will be approximately 7mm x 15cm (⅜in x 6in).

Make the dress as described on page 83, using these ribbons instead.

Make the fringe by cutting a strip of fabric 10cm x 75 cm (4in x 30in), without adding seam allowances. Iron in 6mm (¼in) on each short side, and press the strip in half lengthways so it is 5cm x 74cm (2in x 29½in).

Gather along the open long side and attach the strip to the bottom edge of the dress in the same way as for the Pink Angel's skirt on page 92.

A rose cut from rose-patterned fabric can be ironed onto the dress using double-sided fusible web.

Water Lilies

Pattern can be found on page 148.

YOU WILL NEED:
Fabric for the lily
Fabric for the leaf
Cotton wadding (batting) or similar
A paper flower to embellish, if desired

INSTRUCTIONS:
If you are making the water lily in plain fabric or one with a simple pattern, draw three petals from the pattern overlapping by about 5mm (¼in) on the fabric (see Figure A).

If you want the same look as in the picture, where every petal has the same pattern, draw three half petals next to each other around the pattern details, overlapping them (see Figure B). Remember to draw on the wrong side of the fabric.

You need two identical strips. Sew them together so the pattern is reversed on the lower petals (see Figure C).

You could use a photocopier to enlarge or reduce the pattern. Make sure the pattern parts overlap each other by at least 3mm (⅛in).

Place the whole piece on the fabric for the reverse, right sides together. It is not necessary to put in as much work on the reverse as it will not be visible.

Sew around all three pattern parts to make one connected piece (see Figure D).

Make an opening through the fabric on the reverse using a wooden stick or similar and turn the shape out, easing out the points (see Figure E). Press.

Fold the water lily so the middle of each petal and the joins between the petals are facing down. Sew through all the layers with embroidery yarn (see Figure F). Tighten the thread and sew back and forth a couple of times before you secure the yarn.

Press the tips of the petals so they spread out nicely. You could also sew a few stitches to bring the raised folds in the centre of the lily together. Attach a paper flower or similar to embellish.

Fold the fabric for the leaf right sides together and place wadding (batting) underneath. Trace the pattern and sew around the outline. You will get the best result if you make an opening through one of the layers, but you could also have it in the seam. Turn out, press the leaf and close the opening. Quilt the leaf as marked on the pattern, by hand or machine (see Figure G).

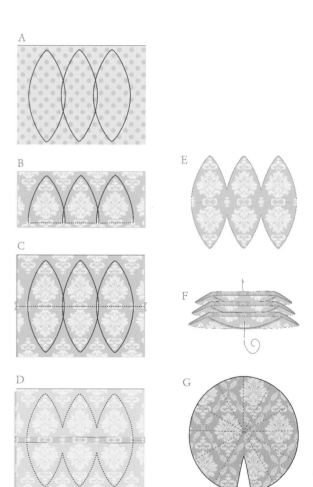

A

B

C

D

E

F

G

Blankets and Cushions

You will see a selection of blankets and cushions in this book. Some are patched, others are made in simple fabrics and then quilted. They are meant to give you inspiration and ideas, so there are no specific instructions for them.

However, here are a few tips:

The easiest way to quilt is to follow a simple geometric pattern, like the diamond shape on the Large Bags on page 77, and the Beauty Bags on page 110. I just followed the pattern on the fabric – easy, straight lines. Even so, this produces a nice effect and gives a more sculpted appearance.

To quilt freehand requires some practice, but you could draw loosely with a disappearing ink pen and then sew over the lines. If you see quilting as an impossible obstacle, you could sew together the patches and then ask a professional quilter to quilt it for you.

You need three layers to sew a quilted cushion cover or blanket – two layers of fabric and one layer of cotton wadding (batting), or similar, in between. The layers should be secured together before quilting, but avoid pins as you will may injure yourself during the quilting. Use safety pins or tacking (basting) stitches in all directions.

Try as much as possible to start in the middle and work your way out to each side. If you sew squares, start by sewing right across the middle of the project and work your way out to one side, then the other. Then turn the project around and do the same thing all over again.

You can sew on a simple piece of fabric to finish a quilt or cushion cover. Border a blanket in the same way as the hats on page 30.

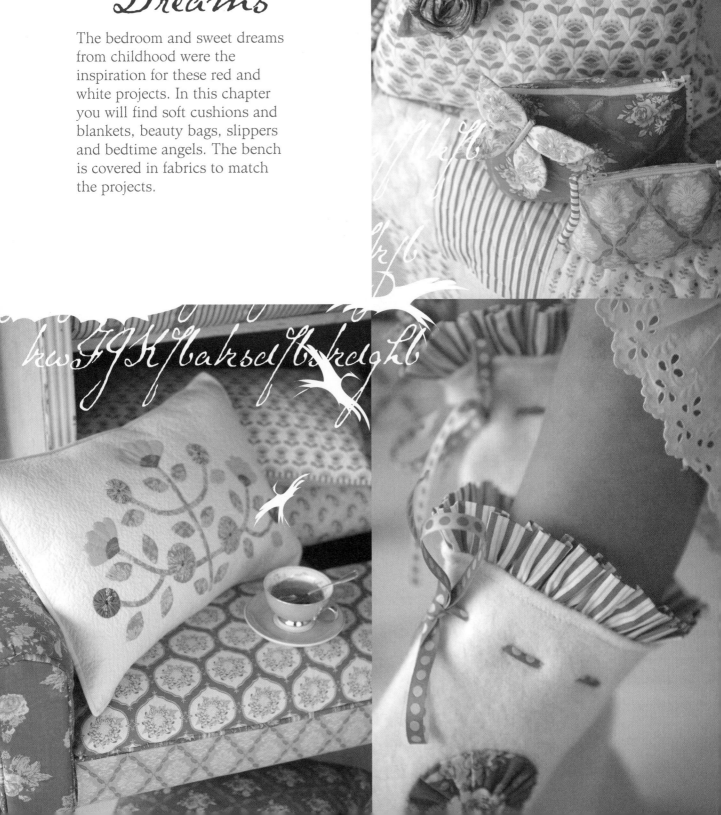

Sweet Dreams

The bedroom and sweet dreams from childhood were the inspiration for these red and white projects. In this chapter you will find soft cushions and blankets, beauty bags, slippers and bedtime angels. The bench is covered in fabrics to match the projects.

Slippers

Pattern can be found on page 148.

YOU WILL NEED:
Wool felt
Fabric for the pleated trim
Ribbon
Embellishments, if desired

INSTRUCTIONS:
Each slipper is made with a lining attached. You will therefore need a piece of felt big enough to take eight pattern pieces to make two slippers. Note that the pattern is in two parts, so you need to match points A and B.

For each slipper, fold half of the felt, right sides together. First draw one slipper from the pattern with the foot facing down. Then reverse the pattern and place it top edge to top edge with the first shape. Draw around it so that the slipper and lining are one piece.

Draw along the dotted lines on the piece that is supposed to be the lining. Mark an opening for turning. Sew around the shape, leaving the areas around the heel and toes open. The slippers will have more flexibility if you use stretch or tiny zigzag stitches.

Cut out the slipper and press the openings at the heel and toes together so the raw edges match and then sew the seams (see Figure B). Turn out the slipper, close the reverse opening and push the lining thoroughly into the slipper. Iron the slipper.

Cut a strip of trim fabric 100cm x 8cm (40in x 3^{1}/4in). Turn under and press 6mm (^{1}/4in) on each of the shortest ends and press the strip in half lengthways. Zigzag stitch the raw edges together. Sew a gathering thread about 6mm (^{1}/4in) down from the zigzag edge. Then gather the trim until it measures the same as the top of the slipper. Sew the pleated trim onto the slipper with zigzag stitch, so about 3cm (1^{1}/4in) is showing above the edge (see Figure C).

Use a small pair of sharp scissors to make holes around the top of the slipper for the ribbon. Make seven holes on each side of the slipper, about 4cm (1^{5}/8in) down from the top of the felt. Thread the ribbon through the holes. For embellishment ideas, see page 16.

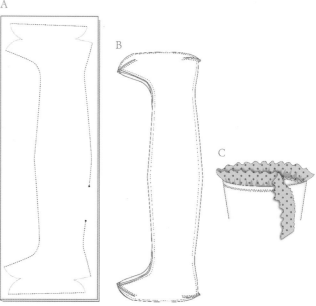

A

B

C

Appliqué

Patterns can be found on page 149.

YOU WILL NEED:
Cushion to appliqué (see page 98)
Various fabrics
Paper or thin card

INSTRUCTIONS:
I used a sewing machine to quilt the whole background fabric for this cushion. It takes some extra time, but gives a beautiful textured look. Those who have the skills can quilt freehand. It's not necessary to quilt, but you should place some wadding (batting) under the fabric to stabilize it before adding the appliqué. The size of the cushion is 55cm x 40cm (20½in x 16in).

The cushion cover has a simple back, comprising of two parts overlapping each other, and a border round the edges.

On the pattern pages you will find patterns for the flower and leaves, a segment of the patterns at full size and a small illustration, which shows you how to put the pattern together.

Use a disappearing ink pen to indicate the pattern on the background fabric. You can measure the spaces between elements if you want. Pin all the shapes in place before sewing the motifs on, so you can adjust them if any are crooked.

BRANCHES

Cut fabric strips measuring 2cm (¾in) wide. Press under about 6mm (¼in) on each side so the strip will be 8mm (⅜in) wide. Pin the strips in place to make the branches.

LEAVES

Cut out leaves from the pattern in paper without a seam allowance. Cut leaves in fabric, adding a seam allowance.

Place a paper leaf against the wrong side of a fabric leaf and fold down one of the fabric tips. Continue to fold over the sides and tack (baste) without sewing in the paper (see Figure A). Continue all around the leaf. Place the leaf on the background and sew on half the leaf. Then wriggle out the paper and sew on the rest of the leaf.

A

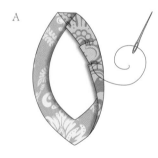

CIRCLES

Cut out two circles measuring 10cm (4in) in diameter, two measuring 8cm (3¼in) and two measuring 7cm (2¾in), adding seam allowances. Make yo-yos as described on page 21.

Place the yo-yos as shown on the pattern and sew in position.

FLOWERS

The pink flowers are sewn from the wrong side because it is difficult to get nice curves folding around paper. Fold a piece of fabric double and trace two small and one large flower from the pattern. Sew around the shapes, leaving an opening at the bottom. Cut out, clipping up to the seam around the curves. Turn out and press. Cut away the seam allowance at the opening. Place the flower on the background. Sew the red part of the flower around the paper, as for the leaves, and place it over the pink petals. Quilt lines on the flowers as marked on the pattern after the flower is sewn to the background.

Bedtime Angels

Patterns can be found on pages 138, 139, 142, 146 and 147.

YOU WILL NEED:
Materials for the angel
(see page 10)
Fabric for the clothes
Thin ribbon to tie the clothes
Ribbon to embellish, if desired

INSTRUCTIONS:
Make the angel as described on page 10, and make hair and face as described on page 13. Sew the cardigan like the wraparound dress on page 83 by following the dotted line marked on the pattern. The trousers are sewn in the same way as pantaloons on page 35.

Beauty Bags and Purses

YOU WILL NEED:
Fabric for the beauty bag
Fabric for the lining
Fabric for the borders
Cotton wadding (batting) or similar
Zipper

INSTRUCTIONS:
Follow the instructions for the Large Bag on page 77 to make the beauty bags and purse, but without the carrying strap and with the measurements given here.

The biggest bag is spacious and works as a toilet bag, the medium is the right size for a makeup bag and the smallest can be used as a purse. The length of the zipper is the same as the top of the bag. Remember to add seam allowances to all the seams.

Large: height 27cm (10⅝in), width on top 27cm (10⅝in), width at the bottom 44cm (17⅜in). 6cm (2⅜in) is folded upwards at the bottom.
Medium: height 17cm (6⅝in), width on top 17cm (6⅝in), width at the bottom 28cm (11in). 4cm (1⅝in) is folded upwards at the bottom.
Small: height 12cm (4¾in), width on top 12cm (4¾in), width at the bottom 20cm (8in). 3cm (1¾in) is folded upwards at the bottom.

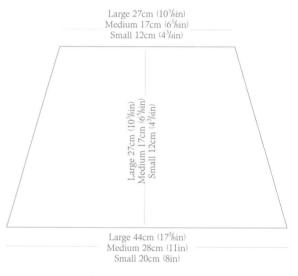

Large 27cm (10⅝in)
Medium 17cm (6⅝in)
Small 12cm (4¾in)

Large 27cm (10⅝in)
Medium 17cm (6⅝in)
Small 12cm (4¾in)

Large 44cm (17⅜in)
Medium 28cm (11in)
Small 20cm (8in)

The Circus

We can't forget the kids – so the circus was the inspiration for this chapter, just for the younger generation. I am particularly fond of the giraffes and elephants, and of course I had to include a circus cockatoo! In this chapter you will also find inspiration for decorating the kids' rooms. Thank you to Oda for her contribution as circus manager!

Circus Tent

The circus tent is sewn a little bit like a tester bed hanging and could be fun to place over a bed.

YOU WILL NEED:
A metal circle or similar
Fabric and linen for the tent canvas
Fabric for the roof
Rope or ribbon as a hanger
Embroidery yarn
Fabric and ribbon to embellish, if desired

INSTRUCTIONS:
I used a metal circle from Panduro Hobby that is used to make lampshades, measuring about 25cm (10in) in diameter. Use whatever you can find.

The fabric for the roof should be 30cm (12in) deep and the width should fit tightly around the circle. Add a seam allowance. Sew in the seam allowance at the bottom. Sew a channel for the rope along the top. 2cm (¾in) for this is already allowed in the 30cm (12in).

To make the channel, press in the corners, press in a 6mm (¼in) seam allowance along the top edge and down. Sew together. Thread the rope through by tying it to a wooden stick and thread the stick through the channel. Fold the roof right sides together, and sew the raw edge closed. Make sure you don't sew into the rope (see Figure A).

Cut two full fabric widths, about 1.5m (1⅔yd) long. (The fabrics I used here are 140cm (54in) wide). Turn and press about 1cm (⅜in) around all of the edges and sew the two fabrics together with the right sides facing out. Pin the top edge into pleats and attach it to the roof for a good fit. It will look best if you fold the pleats in opposite directions on each side of the tent opening (see Figure B). Sew the tent canvas to the roof piece.

Insert the metal circle above the seam between the roof and tent canvas and secure it in place from the outside with embroidery yarn. The border around the edge of the tent will hide the stitches.

A

B

Make the border by folding a strip of patterned fabric right sides together and sewing around the edge. Cut, turn out and press the border. Press in the top edge and sew closed. Attach the border with either adhesive or stitches around the tent. You can attach a ribbon on top if you want. A wide ribbon could also be used to hide the stitches.

Circus Letters

Patterns can be found on pages 150-151.

The circus letters are made out of glitter board you can get in craft stores, but you could also use thick card or similar. Print out the letters on regular paper and glue them to the backside of the glitter rubber board. Cut them out and make at least two holes across the top of each one using a hole punch. Thread the letters onto a string.

Clown Collar

YOU WILL NEED:
Fabric
Ribbons
Embroidery yarn

INSTRUCTIONS:
The large collar fits kids and dogs, the smaller one fits the elephants, giraffes and cockatoos.

Large collar: two fabric widths are sewn together to make a piece approximately 270cm (108in) in length and 26cm (10⅜in) in height.
Cut two ribbons measuring 45cm (18in).

Small collar: 60cm x 10cm (30in x 4in).
Cut two ribbons measuring 25cm (10in).

Add seam allowances to the fabric measurements.

Press under the seam allowances on all sides and then press the collar in half lengthways. Sew the edges together on the short sides and at the same time attach a ribbon on each side, close to the open long side (see Figure A).

Sew a gathering stitch along the open long side with embroidery yarn and adjust to make pleats. Measure the neck of the one wearing the collar before you secure the embroidery yarn.

Take note: The collar should be kept loose for safety reasons.

A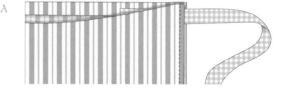

Elephants

Pattern for the large elephant can be found on pages 150–152. Pattern for the small elephant can be found on page 153.

YOU WILL NEED:
Fabric for the body
Lining for the ears
Toy stuffing
Embroidery yarn
Clothes (see pages 124 and 126)
Wadding (batting)

INSTRUCTIONS:
The elephant pattern comes in two sizes. The body for the large elephant is divided in two parts to fit the pattern page. Join the two parts, matching points A and B.

Fold the fabric for body right sides together and trace a body, two legs and two arms from the pattern. Sew around all the parts, except the openings marked with dotted lines on the pattern (see Figure A).

Cut out the parts. Fold the opening in the head together, matching the raw edges and close the opening across the head (see Figure B). Fold the opening at the bottom of the body together and sew the seam closed to create a bottom (see Figure C). Remember to leave an opening for turning.

Close the openings in a similar way across the feet and arms, as shown in Figure D.

Turn out the body through the opening at the bottom and also the legs and arms by making an opening through one of the layers (see Figure E). Press all the parts.

Stuff the body, arms and legs and use a wooden stick or similar to stuff the trunk. Sew together the openings. You could embroider small curved nails on the legs and arms if you want (see Figure F).

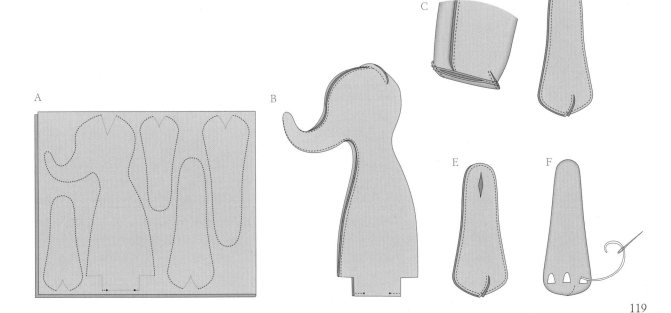

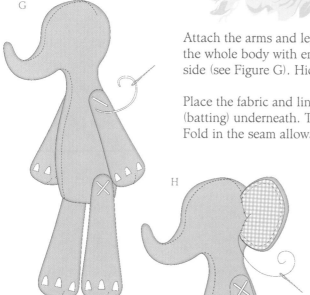

G

H

Attach the arms and legs to the body by sewing back and forth through the whole body with embroidery yarn, finally making a cross on each side (see Figure G). Hide the knots between the arm/leg and body.

Place the fabric and lining for the ears right sides together with wadding (batting) underneath. Trace the ears from the pattern and sew around. Fold in the seam allowance across each opening. You can sew around the ear a little bit from the edge if you want some embellishment. Put extra stuffing into each ear, bend them a little bit and tack them to the head (see Figure H).

Make faces as described on page 13, and clothes as described on pages 124 and 126.

 *Giraffes*

Pattern for the large giraffe can be found on pages 155 and 157. Pattern for the small giraffe can be found on page 154.

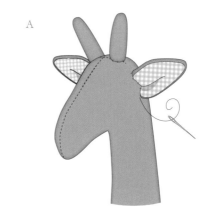

A

YOU WILL NEED:
Fabric for the body
Lining for the ears
Toy stuffing
Embroidery yarn
Clothes (see pages 124 and 126)
Wadding (batting)

INSTRUCTIONS:
The giraffe pattern comes in two different sizes. The body is divided in two parts. Join the two pieces for the body, matching points A and B.

Make the giraffes in the same way as the elephants on page 119. Although the body has a different shape, it has the same openings and the same procedure with two exceptions. Because the giraffes' ears are smaller they don't need any embellishment, so there are no stitches around them.

Also, the giraffes have horns, and you sew them like this:
Fold the fabric for the horns right sides together. Trace the horns from the pattern and sew around. Cut out, use a wooden pin or similar to turn them out and then stuff the horns. Sew the horns and ears as shown in Figure A.

Because the neck needs to be stuffed firmly, it can be a good idea to make the seam around the neck stronger. For the clothes, see pages 124 and 126.

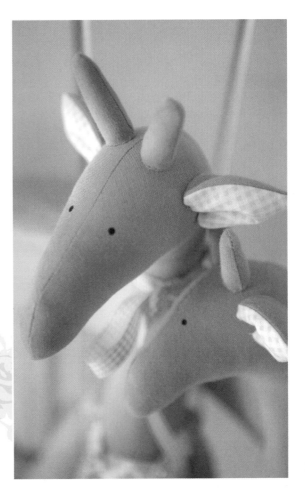

Dungarees

Pattern can be found on pages 156–157.

YOU WILL NEED:
Fabric for the dungarees
Fabric for the pockets
Pearl buttons or beads
Ribbon to embellish, if desired

INSTRUCTIONS:
The dungaree patterns come in two sizes. The large ones fit the large elephant and giraffe while the small ones fit the small animals. Pearl buttons should not be used if there could be any danger of a child choking. Consider the child's age.

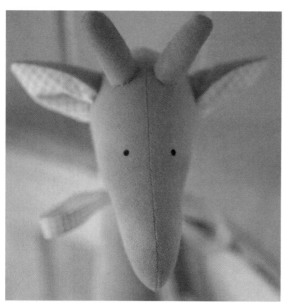

Cut out four identical dungaree parts from the pattern, adding more than enough seam allowance and sew them together two by two (see Figure A). Cut the pockets with a seam allowance, iron in all the edges and sew down the top edge. Fold fabric for the bib right sides together, trace and then sew around it. Cut it out, turn it through and press. Sew the pockets and the bib to the right side of the dungarees front, as shown in Figure B. Place the two pieces for the dungarees right sides together and sew together down each side and between the legs (see Figure C).

Turn the dungarees out. Turn and press the seam allowance around the top and bottom of each leg, pressing the bib upwards. Sew the leg hems. Attach a ribbon around the edge if desired.

Cut two straps measuring 3.5cm x 15 cm (1¼in x 6in), including a seam allowance. Turn and press about 6mm (¼in) on one of the short sides and on each long side. Press the strip in half lengthways and sew together the long open side. The straps will then be about 12mm (½in) wide.

Sew the turned-in ends to each side of the bib with a pearl button or bead. Dress the toy in the dungarees. Fold and sew two tucks in the front of the dungarees and two at the back. Let the straps cross at the back. Pin the straps so you can adjust them until the dungarees look nice before you sew the straps to the back.

A

B

C

Dresses

Pattern can be found on page 158.

YOU WILL NEED:
Fabric for the dress
Ribbon to embellish, if desired

INSTRUCTIONS:
The dress pattern comes in two different sizes. The large dress fits the large elephant and giraffe and the small one fits the small animals. Pearl buttons should not be used if there could be any danger of a child choking. Consider the child's age.

Cut a piece of fabric the size of two dress shapes. Cut out one full shape and two half shapes, as indicated by the vertical dotted line. Place the two half pieces right sides together and sew halfway up from the bottom (see Figure A). Fold out the pieces and sew down the seam allowances on each side of the opening in the seam (see Figure B).

Place the two dress pieces right sides together and sew the side seams. Turn and press the seam allowances along the top and bottom edges. Sew the top seam allowance. If you want, you can attach a ribbon to embellish.

Cut a strip for the skirt of 60cm x 7cm (24in x 2¾in) for the large dress and 50cm x 6cm (20in x 2⅜in) for the small dress. Add more than enough seam allowance. Turn, press and sew the seam allowance at the bottom of the strip. Attach a ribbon to embellish if desired. Fold the strip right sides together again and sew together the side seam. Turn the skirt right side out and sew a gathering stitch around the top edge. Gather the skirt until it fits the dress bodice. Pin the skirt to the bodice (see Figure C).

Dress the toy and sew the opening at the back closed. You could make the two sides overlap each other if the dress is too loose.

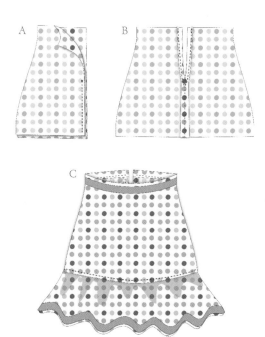

Circus Cushions

Pattern can be found on page 158.

YOU WILL NEED:
Fabric for the skin
Lining for the ear
Fabric for the cushion
Fabric for the pleated frill
Toy stuffing
Wadding (batting)
Ribbon and flower to embellish, if desired

INSTRUCTIONS:
Cut a strip of fabric measuring 42cm x 42cm (17in x 17in) for the front of the cushion. You could back it with fusible interfacing to strengthen it.

Fold the fabric for the circle right sides together and place wadding (batting) underneath. Draw a circle about 16cm (7½in) in diameter by using a plate or something similar and press. Sew around and cut out the circle. Make an opening through one of the layers, turn out and press the circle.

Fold the fabric for the animal right sides together and draw the animal you wish from the pattern. Sew around, leaving an opening at the bottom. Turn out with the help of a wooden pin or similar and press. Fold the seam allowance inwards across the opening and stuff the shape loosely. You could press the animal with an iron and stuff a little more until you have an even but rather flat shape. Sew the animal to the background. Try to make the opening at the bottom follow the curve of the circle, closing the opening.

Make the ears in the same way, using the pattern for the small elephant on page 150, or the small giraffe on page 151. Sew the ears in place.

Cut a strip measuring 10cm (4in), using the whole width of the fabric for the pleated frill. Sew together the short sides and press the strip in half lengthways so it is 5cm (2in) deep. Sew a gathering stitch around the open edges and gather the fabric to create the pleated frill. Attach the frill to the circle so 4cm (1⅝in) is showing (see Figure A). Sew the circle onto the background.

One of the cushion covers is sewn together on the wrong side in the simplest way, and the opening is sewn closed after the pad has been inserted. The other one has got a 2.5cm (1in) wide border with buttons down the side. Cut two strips of 7cm x 44cm (2¾in x 18in), seam allowance included. Iron in 1cm (⅜in) on each short side and press the strips in half lengthways. You could use some thin interfacing to stiffen the strips. Sew buttonholes on one strip and attach buttons on the other. Sew the strips to the front and back of the cushion cover. Place the front and back right sides together and sew together all sides except the side with the button opening (see Figure B).

Make a face as described on page 13. You could also attach a bow made of ribbon and a rose appliqué if desired.

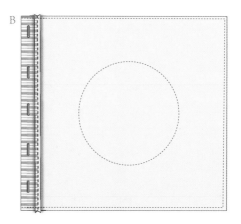

Lollipops

YOU WILL NEED:
Two fabrics
Toy stuffing
Wooden pin
Paper rose, cellophane bag and ribbon, if desired

INSTRUCTIONS:
Cut two squares measuring 15cm x 15cm (6in x 6in) in two different fabrics. Cut diagonally across the fabrics and sew together a triangle from each pattern. Cut diagonally across these (see Figure A). Put one sewn-together triangle from each, set aside and sew the remaining parts together as shown in Figure B. Cut across these pieces in both directions (see Figure C). Rotate two of the pieces and sew the square back together (see Figure D). Make a second lollipop with the remaining pieces.

The backing for the lollipops is made with a simple fabric. Cut a piece of backing fabric and place it right sides together with a pieced square. Draw a circle – the lollipops shown opposite are about 10cm (4in) in diameter. Sew around and leave an opening at the edge. Cut and turn out, press and stuff the lollipop. Twist a wooden pin inside the lollipop and sew the opening around the pin closed.

If you want to embellish the lollipops, you could glue on a small motif and put a cellophane bag over the lollipop. Tie the cellophane in place with a ribbon bow.

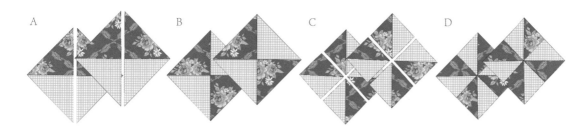

A   B   C   D

Hairband

You can make a cute hairband by dressing an ordinary plastic hairband in fabric and attaching a large rose (page 19). Plastic hairbands can be bought from Panduro Hobby.

131

Candy Cushion

YOU WILL NEED:
Two fabrics for the cushion top
Fabric for the sides and bottom
Fabric for the pleated frills
Fusible interfacing
Toy stuffing

INSTRUCTIONS:
Cut two squares of fabric 45cm x 45cm (18in x 18in), make the candy pattern in the same way as for the lollipop on page 131. You only need one finished square for the cushion top. Bond fusible interfacing to the wrong side of the square.

Draw a large circle that measures 30–40cm (12–16in) in diameter centred on the square. Use a round plate or similar to help. Cut out the circle, adding a seam allowance.

Cut two rectangles, each big enough for half the circle plus extra seam allowance. Bond interfacing to both rectangles and place them right sides together. Sew the rectangles together along one of the long sides, but leave a 15cm (6in) opening in the middle of the seam (see Figure A). Open the square out, draw a circle to match the cushion top and cut out with a seam allowance.

Cut a strip 14cm (5⅝in) deep and the same length as the circumference of the cushion top. Add a seam allowance. Bond interfacing to the wrong side.

Cut two strips measuring 6cm (2½in), using the whole fabric width – here I used fabric 140cm (54in) wide. Sew the short sides on each strip together, and press the strips in half lengthways so they are 3cm (1¼in) deep. Sew a gathering stitch along the open side, gathering the fabric to make pleats. Fit the frill to the cushion circle, a little bit in from the edge. Sew one pleated frill to the bottom circle and one to the top circle with a zigzag stitch all the way out at the edge (see Figure B).

Place the side strip right sides together with the top circle and sew them together around the edge (see Figure C). Then sew the bottom circle to the other end in the same way. Sew together the short sides of the strip. Trim the seam allowance. Turn the cushion cover through the opening at the bottom and stuff it before you close the opening.

A

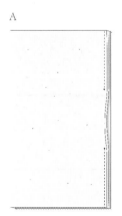

B

C

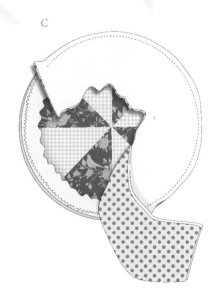

132

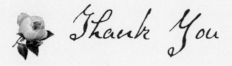 *Thank You*

Sølvi Dos Santos

Sølvi is an amazing photographer. She travels all the way from Paris to our windy little island in Norway to set up cute angels with international elegance. She is also a wonderful person.

Ingrid Skaansar

Ingrid has contributed to most of the Tilda books and without her we wouldn't know what to do. She is not only good company, but also a great stylist who has contributed to the whole of Tilda. She is a methodical person with exceptional memory and drive.

Bodil Haga

This designer got the challenging task of putting this book together. This was a difficult job with all the different elements – pictures, illustrations and text in addition to the author's strong opinions. Thank you for doing a great job and for the pleasant communication.

Tom Undhjem

Tom brings his knowledge, experience and enthusiasm to a whole new level and has been an important contributor to this book. Thank you for the effort.

Karin Mundal

My patient publisher at Cappelen Damm. Thank you for another great collaboration.

Tilla

The model who would rather work but got pushed in front of the camera instead because she is so beautiful. Not many people dare to have Kikko the cockatoo on their shoulders and at the same time have a relaxed smile!

Oda

Our beautiful model in the circus room – she was modelling as if she had been doing it for years.

Eirin

Essential assistant with a bright head and an untiring drive.

Anette Berntsen

The hairdresser who showed up at short notice every time we needed her steady hand and has made the most beautiful hairstyles in this book.

Torje

For her help, patience and support.

Totto & Kikko

Our "children" – the dog and the cockatoo – who modelled for Mom.

 *Props*

LandRomAntikk

As usual LandRomAntikk helped with great eagerness. They now how a new store in Tønsberg located in Nedre Langgate 43, 3126 Tønsberg, (telephone: 41 34 19 68) and have an online store at www.landromantikk.no

NoaNoa

They are located at Storgaten 39, 3126 Tønsberg, (telephone: 33 31 99 00). Visit their website at www.noanoa.com

Mowe

They are located at Storgaten 42, 3126 Tønsberg, (telephone: 33 31 86 40).

Kremmerhuset

They are located at Jernbanegata 1D, 3110 Tønsberg, (telephone: 91 68 16 74). Visit their website at www.kremmerhuset.no

See page 8 for the materials used in the projects.

# Patterns

The page reference for the pattern is on the instruction page for the project.

Take note: Seam allowances need to be added to all of the the patterns except where marked with a dotted line (see below).

On areas marked with a dashed line, add a regular to larger seam allowance. The line shows where two parts of a pattern have to be joined; these are indicated by A and B points, which need to be matched.

Wool felt does not ravel, so it is not necessary to have seam allowances along openings or open edges. These are also marked with a dotted line and should be cut on the pattern line.

SYMBOLS

ES means "extra seam allowance", which is extra important where indicated. Fold under the inner dotted line, if you are not joining to another piece, like on legs on the angel. Always sew across seam allowances that end by an opening.

Dashed lines mark openings, matching lines (for example when joining two fabrics or pattern pieces together) or stitch details.

Dotted lines mark edges that can be cut right off.

Fold means that the pattern should be cut out with the marked edge on the fold of the fabric to give the whole shape.

Illustrations for Iron-on Décor on page 73
Copyright Tone Finnanger

137

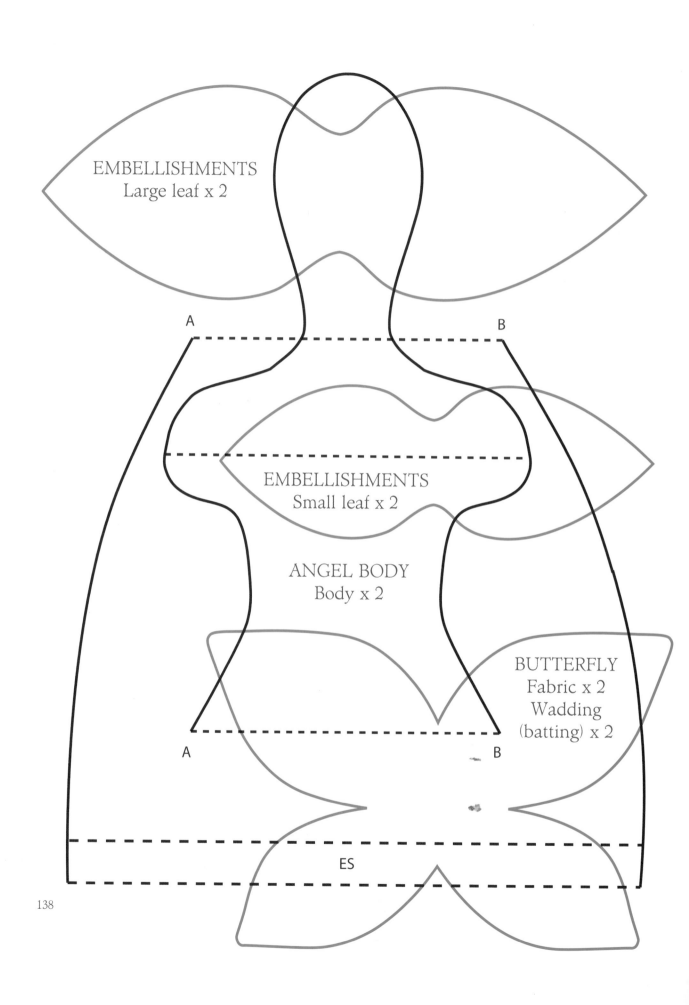

EMBELLISHMENTS
Large leaf x 2

A

B

EMBELLISHMENTS
Small leaf x 2

ANGEL BODY
Body x 2

BUTTERFLY
Fabric x 2
Wadding
(batting) x 2

A

B

ES

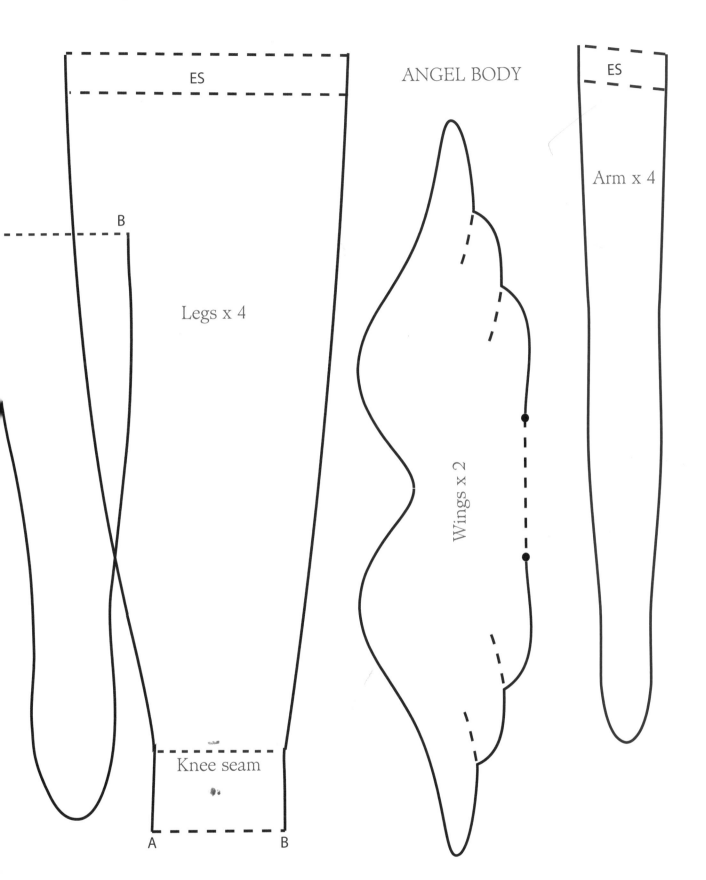

ES

ANGEL BODY

ES

Arm x 4

B

Legs x 4

Wings x 2

Knee seam

A   B

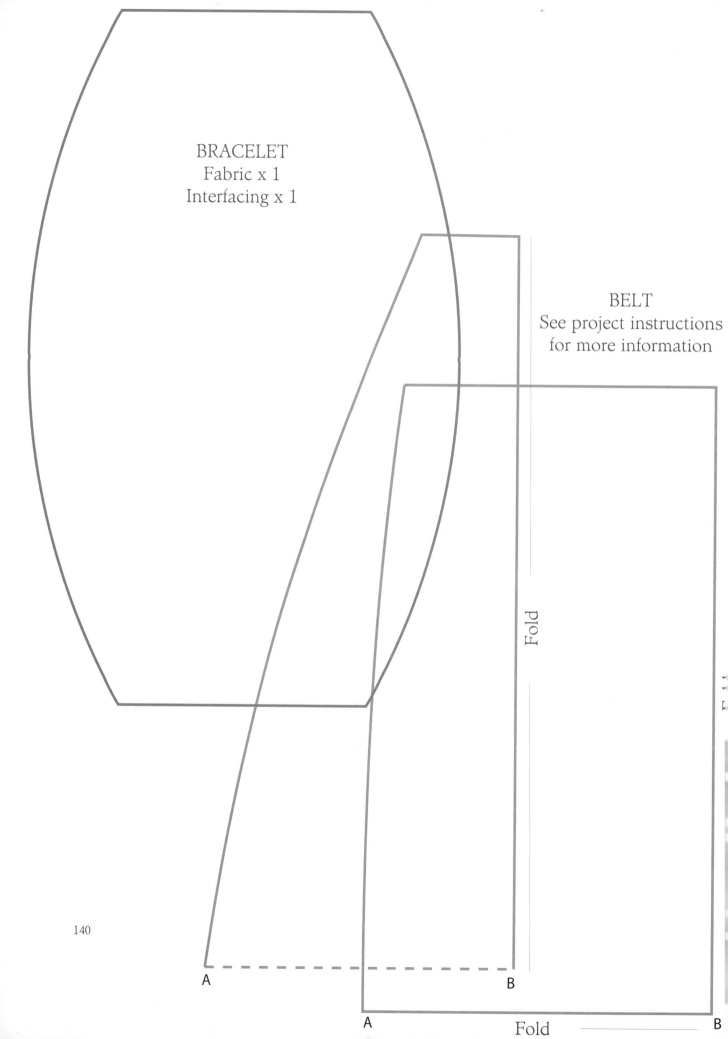

BRACELET
Fabric x 1
Interfacing x 1

BELT
See project instructions
for more information

Fold

140

A

B

A

Fold

B

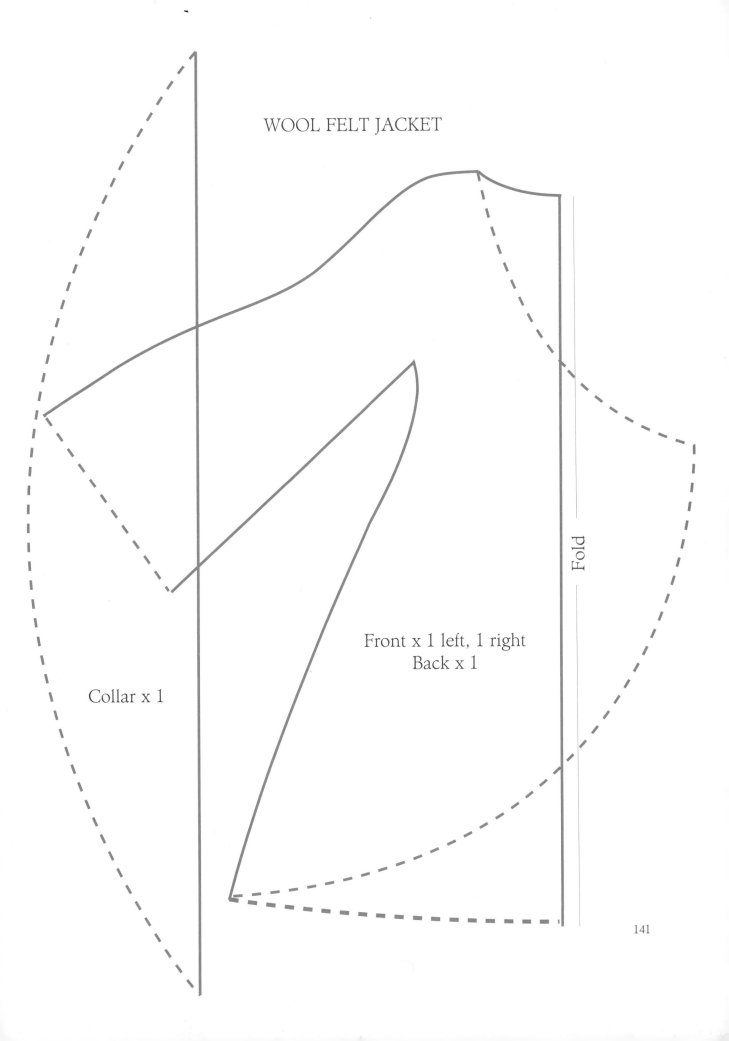

WOOL FELT JACKET

Collar x 1

Front x 1 left, 1 right
Back x 1

Fold

141

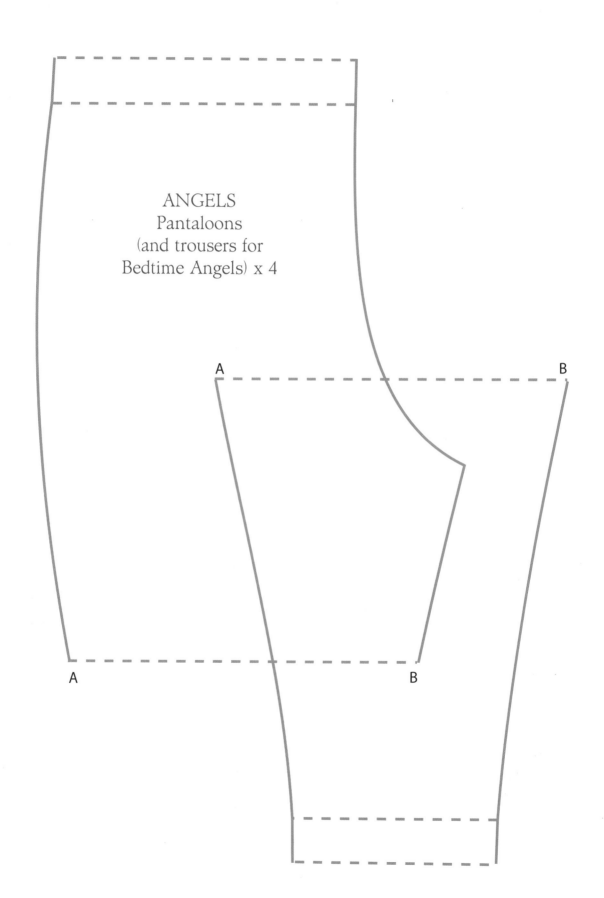

ANGELS
Pantaloons
(and trousers for
Bedtime Angels) x 4

A

B

A

B

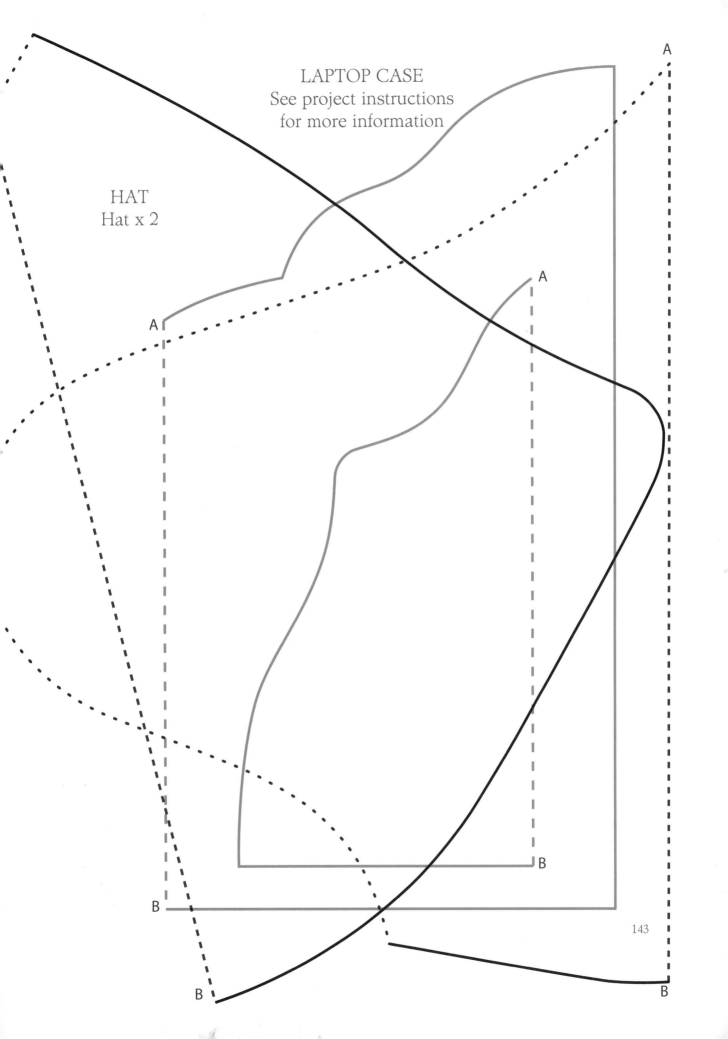

LAPTOP CASE
See project instructions
for more information

HAT
Hat x 2

A

A

A

A

B

B

B

B

143

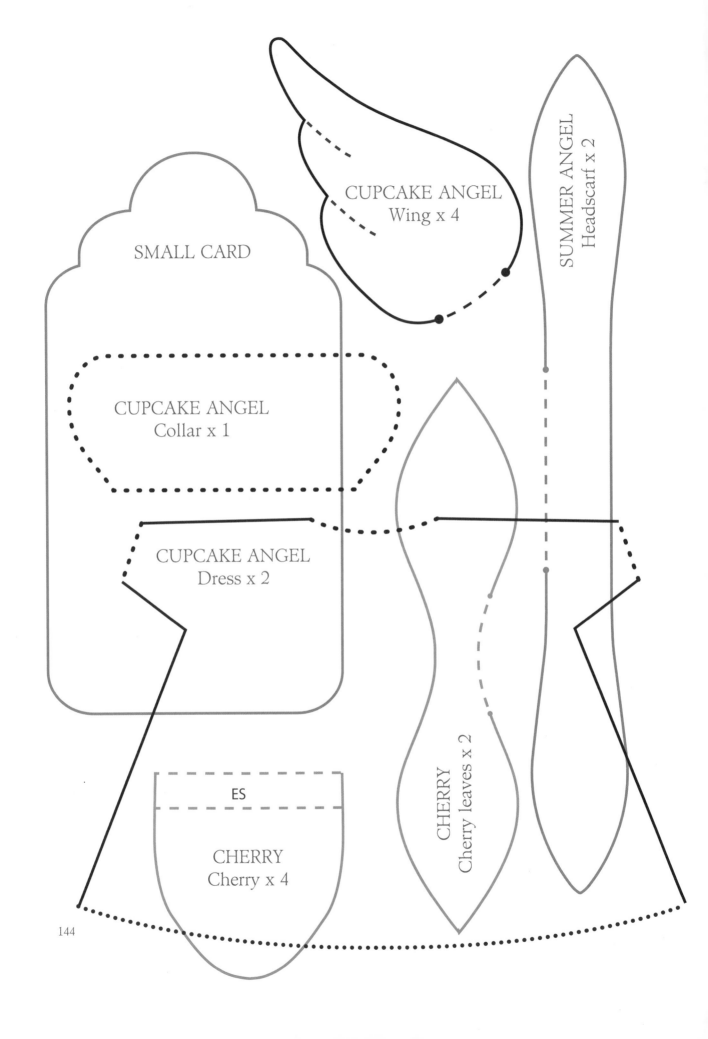

SMALL CARD

CUPCAKE ANGEL
Wing x 4

SUMMER ANGEL
Headscarf x 2

CUPCAKE ANGEL
Collar x 1

CUPCAKE ANGEL
Dress x 2

CHERRY
Cherry leaves x 2

ES

CHERRY
Cherry x 4

144

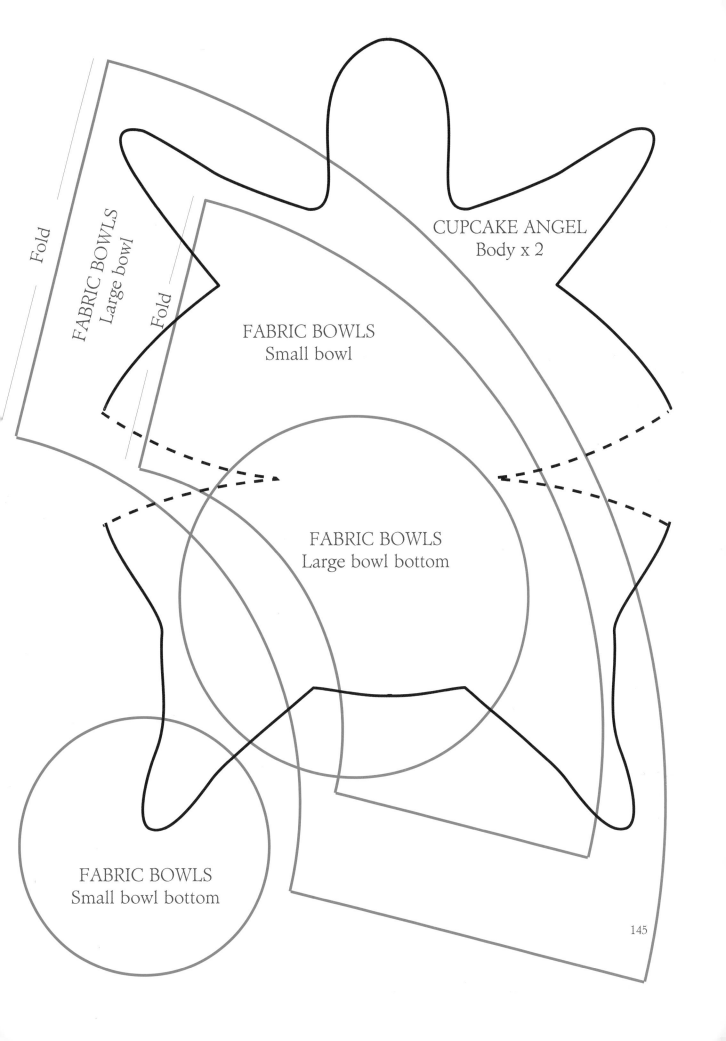

FABRIC BOWLS
Large bowl

Fold

Fold

FABRIC BOWLS
Small bowl

CUPCAKE ANGEL
Body x 2

FABRIC BOWLS
Large bowl bottom

FABRIC BOWLS
Small bowl bottom

145

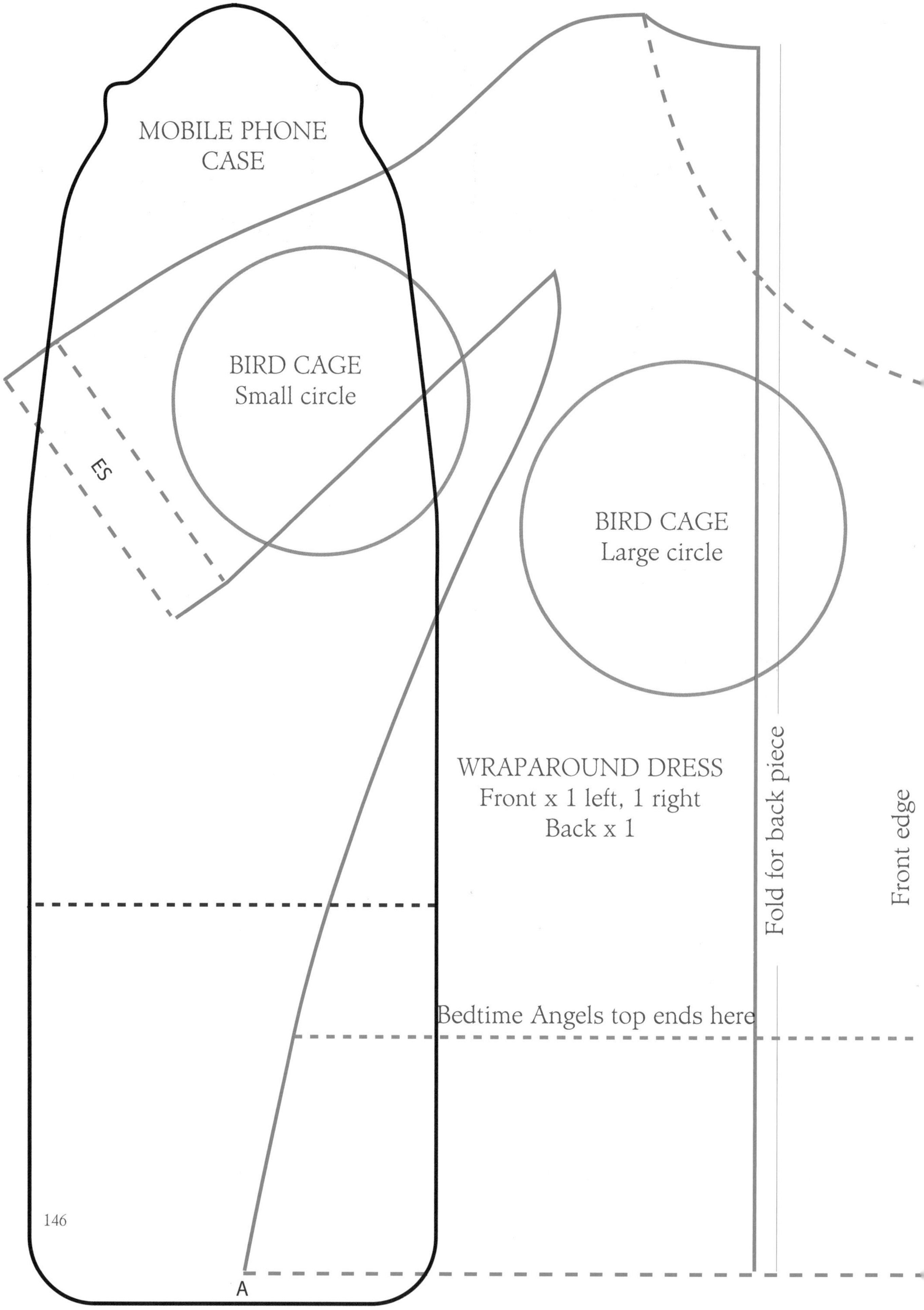

MOBILE PHONE
CASE

BIRD CAGE
Small circle

ES

BIRD CAGE
Large circle

WRAPAROUND DRESS
Front x 1 left, 1 right
Back x 1

Fold for back piece

Front edge

Bedtime Angels top ends here

A

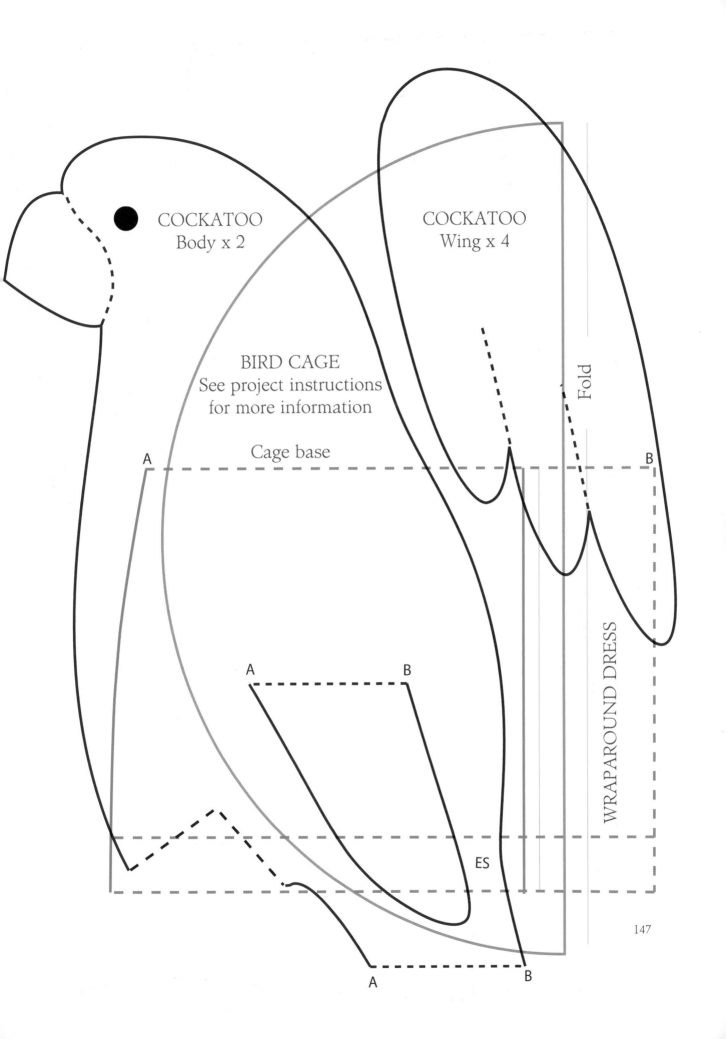

COCKATOO
Body x 2

COCKATOO
Wing x 4

BIRD CAGE
See project instructions
for more information

Cage base

A

B

Fold

A

B

ES

WRAPAROUND DRESS

A

B

147

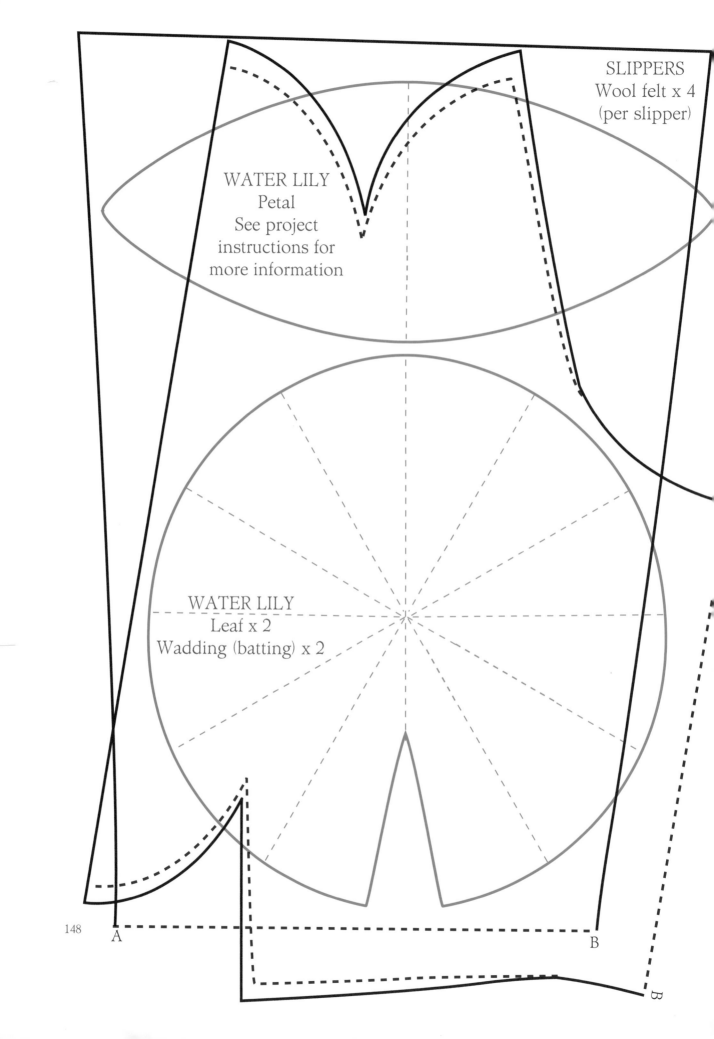

SLIPPERS
Wool felt x 4
(per slipper)

WATER LILY
Petal
See project
instructions for
more information

WATER LILY
Leaf x 2
Wadding (batting) x 2

148

A

B

B

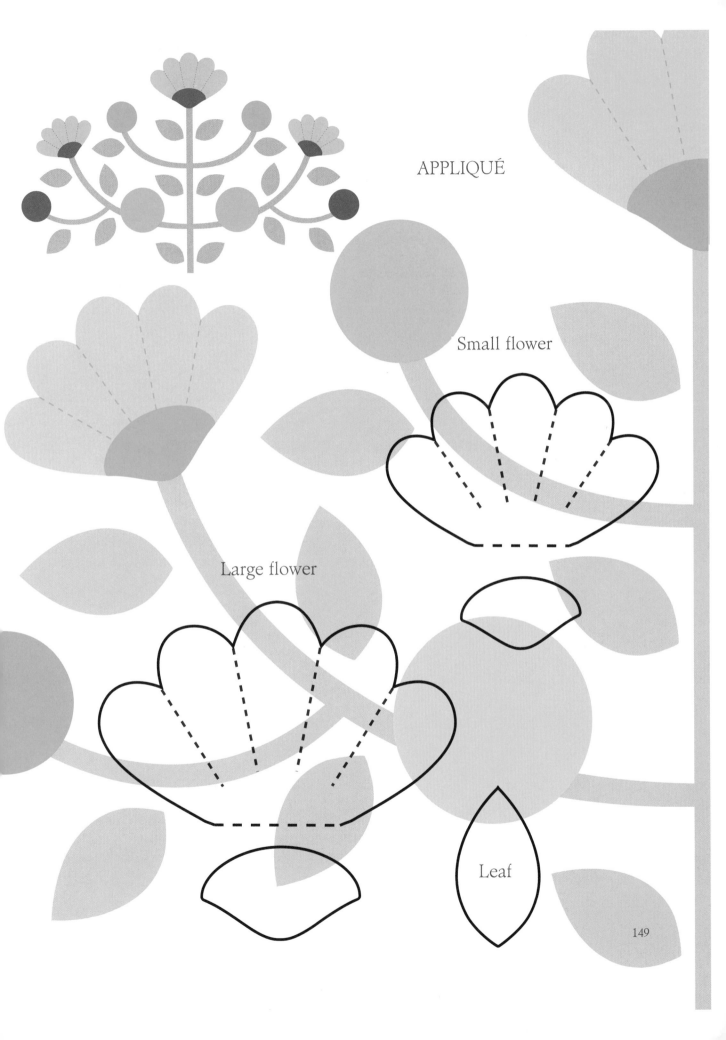

APPLIQUÉ

Small flower

Large flower

Leaf

149

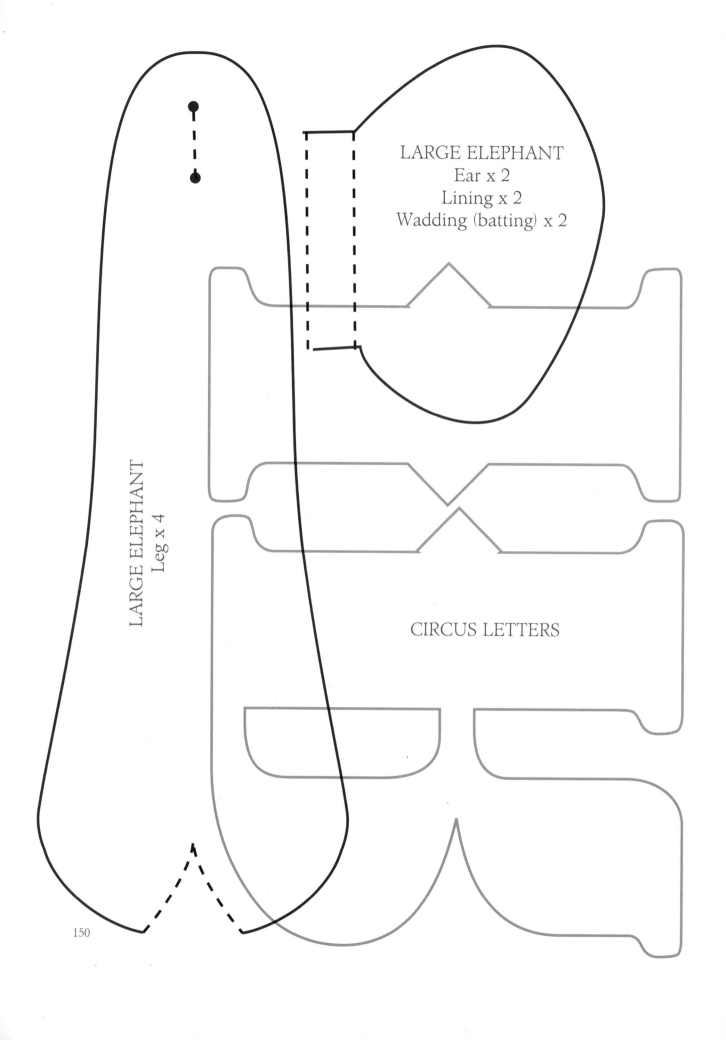

LARGE ELEPHANT
Ear x 2
Lining x 2
Wadding (batting) x 2

LARGE ELEPHANT
Leg x 4

CIRCUS LETTERS

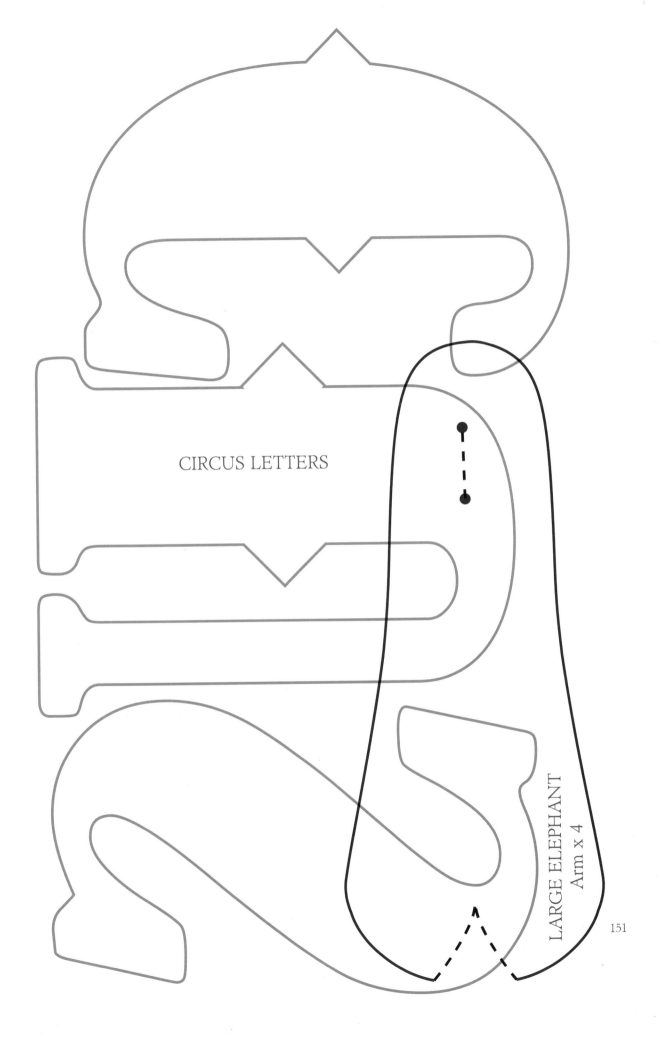

CIRCUS LETTERS

LARGE ELEPHANT
Arm x 4

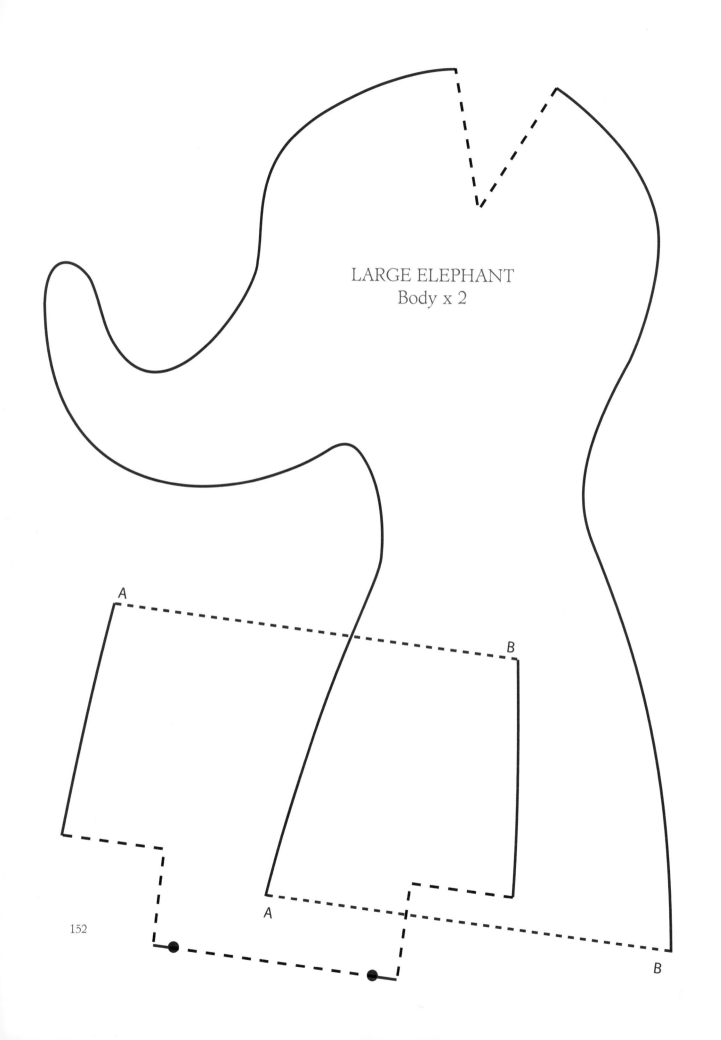

LARGE ELEPHANT
Body x 2

A

B

A

B

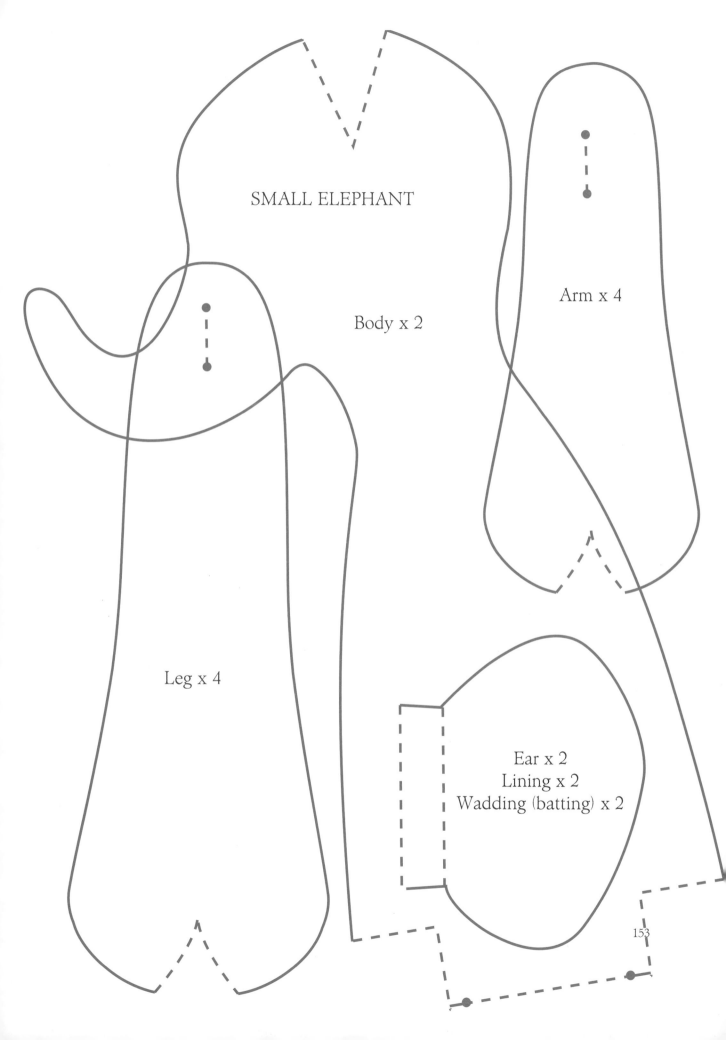

SMALL ELEPHANT

Body x 2

Arm x 4

Leg x 4

Ear x 2
Lining x 2
Wadding (batting) x 2

153

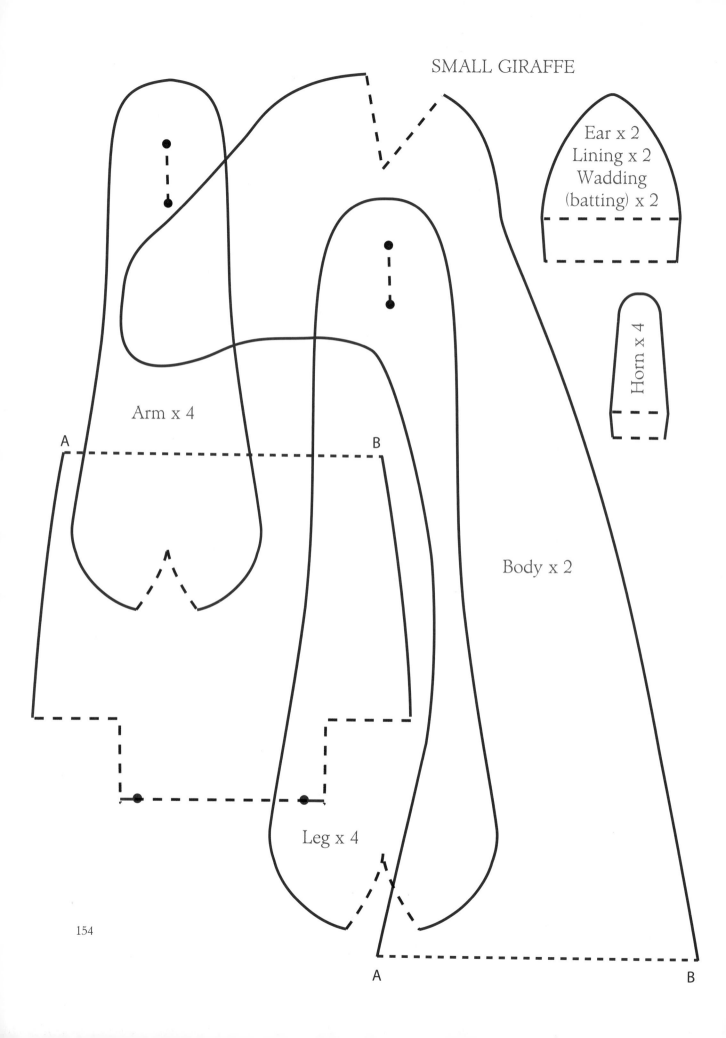

SMALL GIRAFFE

Ear x 2
Lining x 2
Wadding
(batting) x 2

Horn x 4

Arm x 4

A   B

Body x 2

Leg x 4

A   B

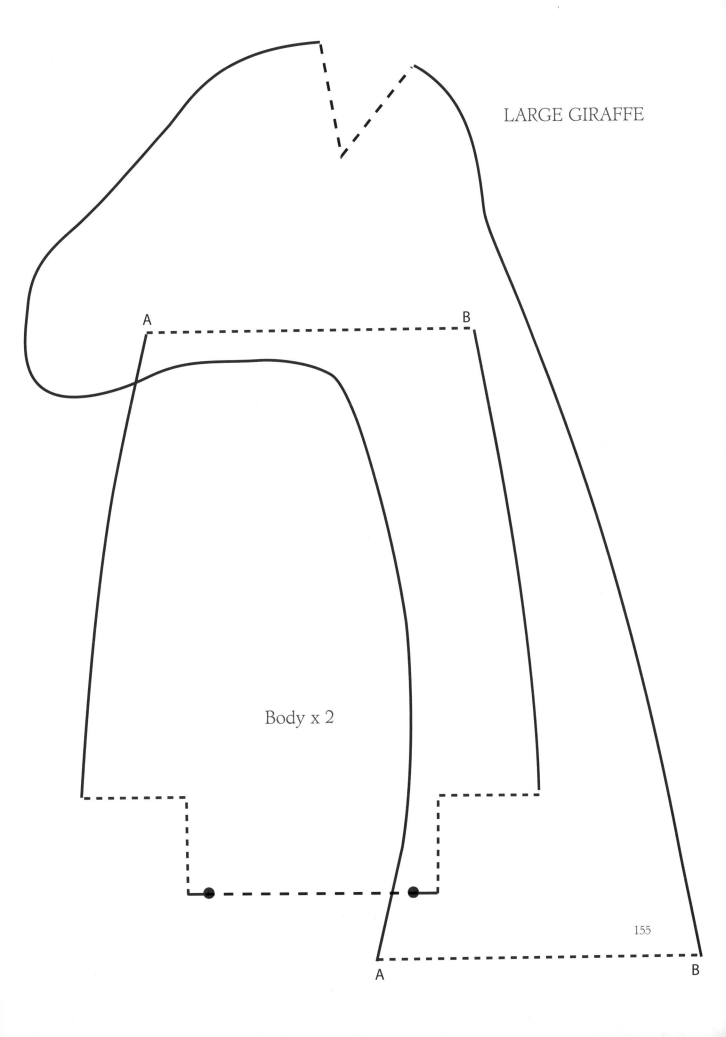

LARGE GIRAFFE

A

B

Body x 2

155

A

B

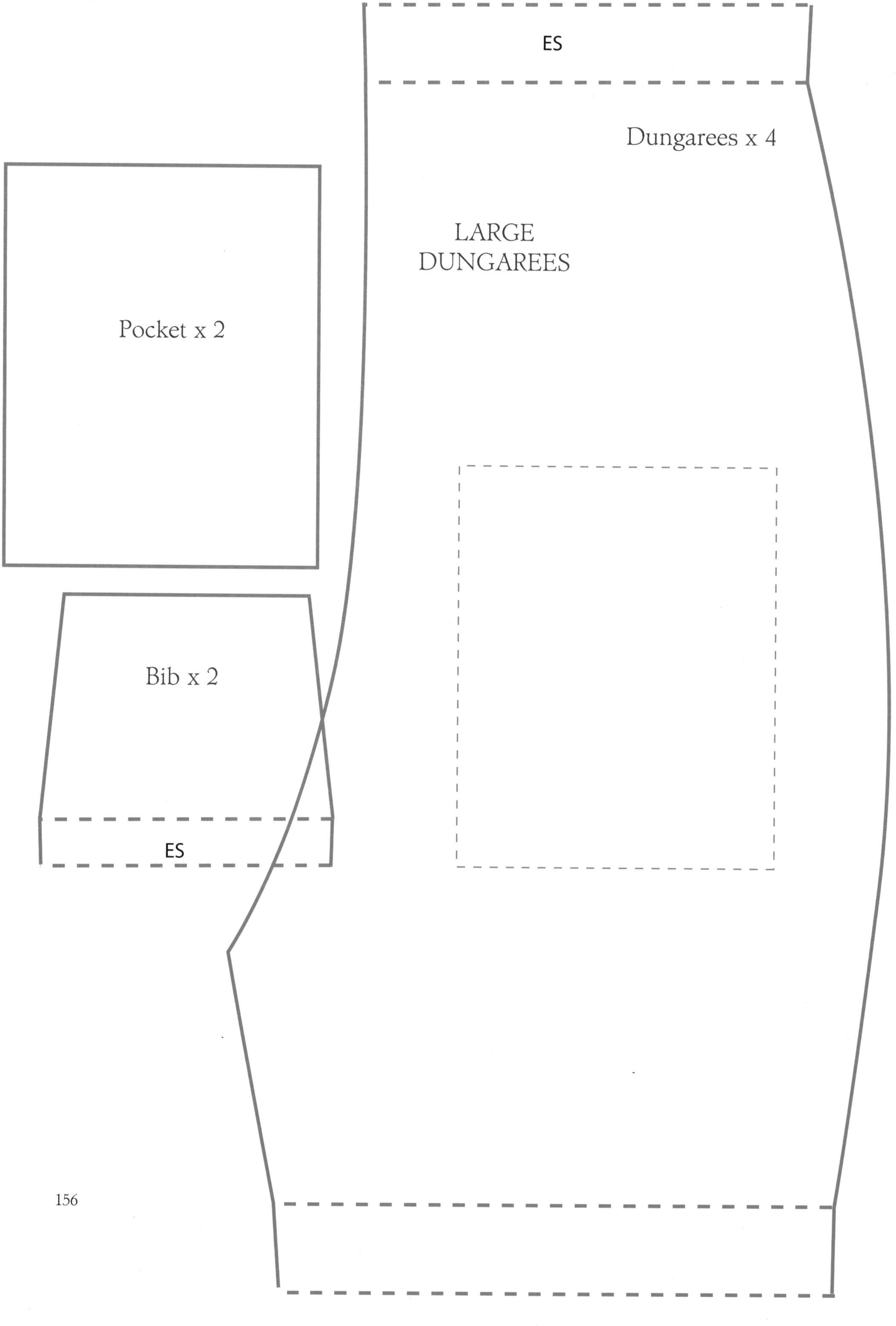

ES

Dungarees x 4

LARGE
DUNGAREES

Pocket x 2

Bib x 2

ES

SMALL DUNGAREES

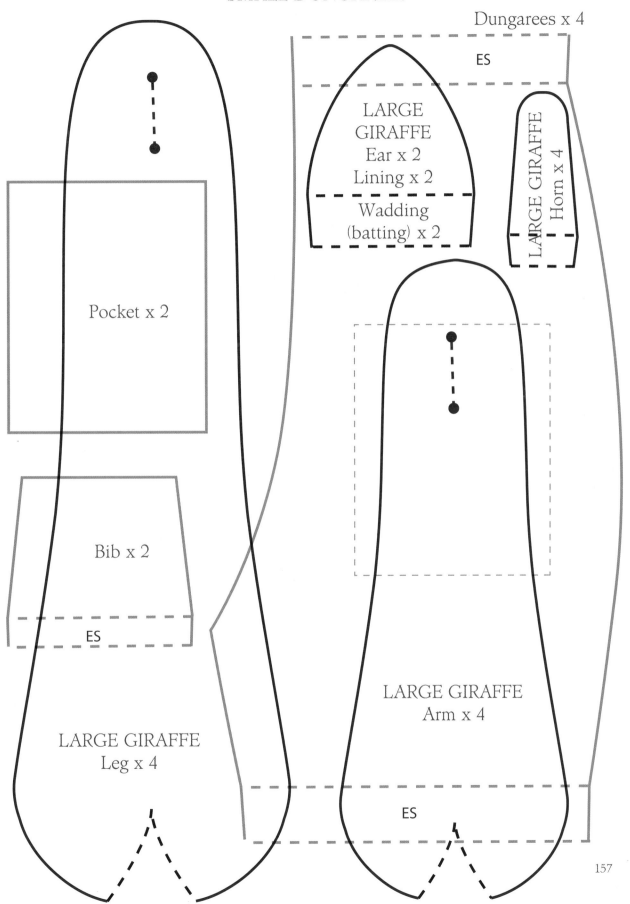

Dungarees x 4

ES

LARGE
GIRAFFE
Ear x 2
Lining x 2

Wadding
(batting) x 2

LARGE GIRAFFE
Horn x 4

Pocket x 2

Bib x 2

ES

LARGE GIRAFFE
Arm x 4

LARGE GIRAFFE
Leg x 4

ES

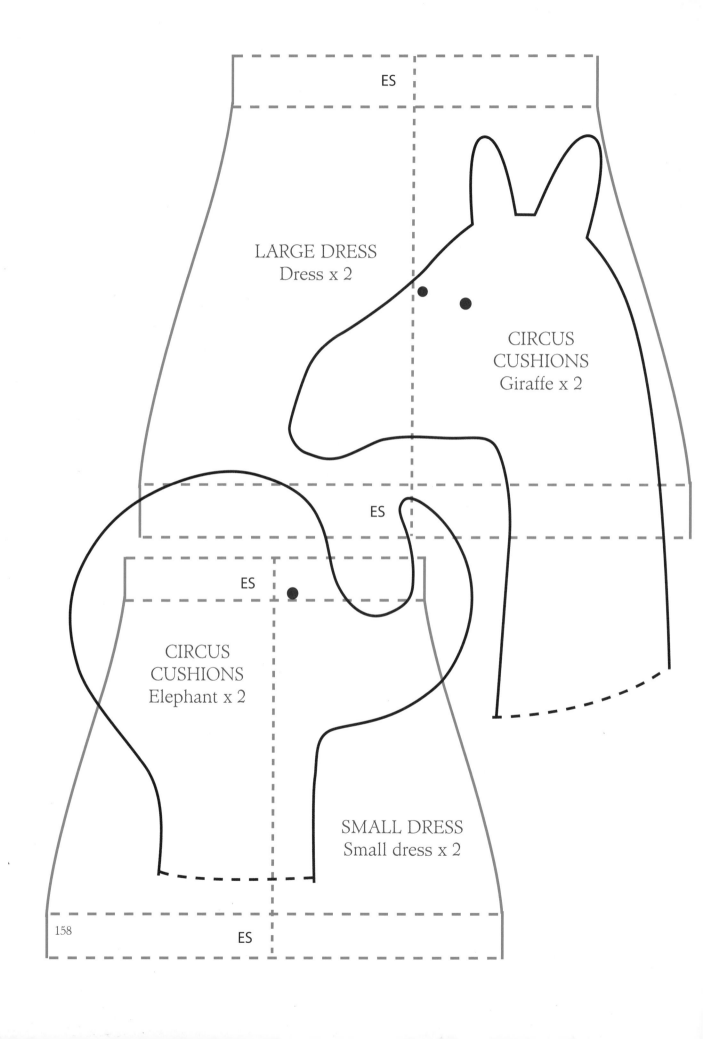

LARGE DRESS
Dress x 2

ES

CIRCUS
CUSHIONS
Giraffe x 2

ES

CIRCUS
CUSHIONS
Elephant x 2

ES

SMALL DRESS
Small dress x 2

ES

Suppliers

UK

Panduro Hobby
Westway House
Transport Avenue
Brentford
Middlesex
TW8 9HF
Tel: 020 8566 1680
trade@panduro.co.uk
www.pandurohobby.co.uk

Coast and Country Crafts
8 Sampson Gardens
Ponsanooth
Truro
Cornwall
TR3 7RS
Tel: 01872 863894
www.coastandcountrycrafts.co.uk

Threads and Patches
48 Aylesbury Street
Fenny Stratford
Bletchley
Milton Keynes
MK2 2BU
Tel: 01908 649687
www.threadsandpatches.co.uk

The Cotton Patch
1283-1285 Stratford Road
Hall Green
Birmingham
B28 9AJ
Tel: 0121 702 2840
www.cottonpatch.co.uk

Puddlecrafts
7 St. Clair Park
Route Militaire
St. Sampson
Guernsey
GY2 4DX
Tel: 01481 245441
www.puddlecrafts.co.uk

The Fat Quarters
5 Choprell Road
Blackhall Mill
Newcastle
NE17 7TN
Tel: 01207 565728
www.thefatquarters.co.uk

Fred Aldous Ltd.
37 Lever Street
Manchester
M1 1LW
Tel: 08707 517301
www.fredaldous.co.uk

The Sewing Bee
52 Hillfoot Street
Dunoon
Argyll
PA23 7DT
Tel: 01369 706879
www.thesewingbee.co.uk

USA

Coats and Clark USA
PO Box 12229
Greenville
SC29612-0229
Tel: 1 800 648 1479
www.coatsandclark.com

Keepsake Quilting
Box 1618
Center Harbor
NH 03226
Tel: 1 800 525 8086
www.keepsakequilting.com

The City Quilter
157 West 24th Street
New York
NY 1011
Tel: 1 212 807 0390
www.cityquilter.com

Connecting Threads
13118 NE 4th Street
Vancouver
WA 9884
Tel: 1 800 574 6454
www.connectingthreads.com

The Craft Connection
21055 Front Street
PO Box 1088
Onley
VA 23418
Tel: 1 888 204 4050
www.craftconn.com

eQuilter
5455 Spine Road
Suite E
Boulder
CO 80301
Tel: 1 877 322 7423
www.equilter.com

Hamels Fabrics
5843 Lickman Road
Chilliwack
British Columbia
V2R 4B5
Tel: 1 877 774 2635
www.hamelsfabrics.com

JoAnn Stores Inc.
5555 Darrow Road
Hudson
OH 44236
Tel: 1 888 739 4120
www.joann.com

Pink Chalk Fabrics
9723 Coppertop Loop
Suite 205
Bainbridge Island
WA 98110
Tel: 1 888 894 0658
www.pinkchalkfabrics.com

Index